Text & Teaching

This volume is one of a series of publications resulting from the Bicentennial celebration of Georgetown University (1789–1989). Publication of this series has been made possible in large part through a gift from Mrs. John R. Gaines. Her assistance and generosity is acknowldged with gratitude and appreciation.

Text & Teaching
The Search for Human Excellence

MICHAEL J. COLLINS **and** FRANCIS J. AMBROSIO
Editors

GEORGETOWN UNIVERSITY PRESS

Georgetown University Press, Washington, D.C. 20057
Copyright © 1991 by Georgetown University Press. All rights reserved.
PRINTED IN THE UNITED STATES OF AMERICA
10 9 8 7 6 5 4 3 2 1   1991
THIS VOLUME IS PRINTED ON ACID-FREE ∞ OFFSET BOOK PAPER.

Library of Congress Cataloging-in-Publication Data

Text and teaching : the search for human excellence / edited by Michael J.
   Collins and Francis J. Ambrosio
       p.   cm.
   Based on papers presented at a symposium held at Georgetown
University, in Washington, D.C., in Oct. 1985 and Sept. 1989.
     1. Literature--Study and teaching (Higher)--United States-
-Congresses. I. Collins, Michael J., 1941-   . II. Francis J. Ambrosio,
1949- .
PN70.T48   1991   807'.1'173--dc20   91-43554
ISBN 0-87840-529-1 (pbk.)

Contributors

Francis J. Ambrosio is Associate Professor of Philosophy at Georgetown University.

William J. Bennett has served as Chairman of the National Endowment for the Humanities, United States Secretary of Education, and Director of the Office of National Drug Control Policy. He is now Senior Editor of The National Review.

William J. Brennan, Jr. served thirty-four terms as Associate Justice of the United States Supreme Court and is now Visiting Professor at Georgetown's Law School. He retired in 1990.

Kevin M. Cahill, M.D., is Director of the Tropical Disease Center at Lenox Hill Hospital in New York City and Professor and Chairman of the Department of International Health and Tropical Medicine at the Royal College of Surgeons in Dublin.

Michael J. Collins is Dean of the School for Summer and Continuing Education at Georgetown University.

Athol Fugard is an internationally acclaimed playwright, actor, director, and filmmaker. He was awarded the degree of Doctor of Humane Letters (*honoris causa*) by Georgetown University in 1984.

Howard J. Gray, S.J., has served as Dean of the Weston School of Theology in Massachusetts and Provincial of the Detroit Province of the Society of Jesus. He is currently Director of Tertianship for the Province.

William H. Gray III, of Pennsylvania, who will complete his seventh term in the House of Representatives in 1992, has been chosen President of the United Negro College Fund.

Timothy S. Healy, S.J., served as President of Georgetown University for fourteen years. He resigned in 1989 to become President of the New York Public Library.

Nancy Landon Kassebaum is currently serving her third term as United States Senator from Kansas.

Edmund D. Pellegrino, M.D., a former President of The Catholic University of America, now serves as Director of the Kennedy Institute of Ethics and John Carroll Professor of Medicine and Medical Humanities at Georgetown University.

Renée Poussaint, an Emmy-award winning journalist, currently co-anchors WJLA's evening and late night news on Channel 7 in Washington, D.C. She was awarded the degree of Doctor of Humane Letters (*honoris causa*) by Georgetown University in 1989.

William J. Richardson, S.J., is Professor of Philosophy at Boston College.

James B. Stockdale, Vice Admiral, United States Navy (retired), has served as President of the Naval War College and The Citadel. He is currently Senior Research Fellow at The Hoover Institution, Stanford University.

William F. Winter served as Governor of Mississippi from 1980 to 1984. He now practices law in Jackson, Mississippi.

Contents

Preface ix

Introduction xiii
  Timothy S. Healy, S.J.

The Book of Job 1
  Edmund D. Pellegrino, M.D.

Plato's Republic 17
  William J. Bennett

Sophocles' Antigone 25
  Nancy Landon Kassebaum

Epictetus' Enchiridion 31
  James Bond Stockdale

Teaching Epictetus 45
  William J. Richardson, S.J.

Machiavelli's The Prince 51
  Renée Poussaint

The Spiritual Exercises of St. Ignatius Loyola 69
  Howard J. Gray, S.J.

Shakespeare's King Lear 85
  Michael J. Collins

The Essays of Ralph Waldo Emerson 101
  William Winter

Henry David Thoreau's Walden   109
   Athol Fugard

The Collected Poems of William Butler Yeats   125
   Kevin M. Cahill, M.D.

Martin Luther King's Why We Can't Wait   139
   William H. Gray III

The Constitution of the United States   149
   William J. Brennan, Jr.

Preface

In October, 1985, and again, at the opening of its Bicentennial celebration in September, 1989, Georgetown University welcomed to its campus a group of accomplished men and women to take part in a Symposium on Text and Teaching. Each of these distinguished guests was asked to discuss, with an audience of alumni, students, and members of the faculty, some classic text: a book, an essay, a poem, a play, a philosophical or legal document that had made an impact on his or her life. The essays gathered in this volume are (with three exceptions) essentially transcriptions of those discussions, the reflections of accomplished men and women on texts that have spoken profoundly and significantly to them. As their words make clear, the texts they chose have in some way defined for them a vision by which they hope to live and have provided them the insight, the inspiration, and the encouragement to act, in both their personal and professional lives, wisely and justly.

* * *

For just over two hundred years now, Georgetown University has drawn to a hilltop overlooking the City of Washington countless young men and women—from the Republic whose history runs concurrently with its own and from virtually every country in the world. It has, during those two centuries, continually invited its students to read, discuss, and ponder the enduring words by which other men and women have expressed their hopes and fears, their dreams and visions, their values and beliefs. And it has done so because it believes that the heart of a liberal education rests in an engagement of the past with the present, in the encounter of an individual with a classic text.

x   PREFACE

The Symposia on Text and Teaching, then, were meant to reflect and celebrate Georgetown's way of teaching and learning, to reaffirm, through the witness of successful men and women, its faith that the texts its teachers and students read together may speak, with wisdom and power, over a lifetime, that they may make possible, to use the words of Socrates, an examination of their lives so as to discover how they might live, wisely and justly, on a fragile planet, in the company of other men and women, the only lives they are given to live. We publish the discussions here so that they might instigate new encounters between readers and texts, encounters that will perhaps shape visions, direct lives, or, at least, bring encouragement and hope.

* * *

In addition to the distinguished speakers, the first Symposium on Text and Teaching brought to Georgetown teachers and administrators from colleges and universities around the country. Among them was Judy Anderson Gordon, a teacher of reading and President of the Education Association at the Hinds Community College District near Jackson, Mississippi. Using Georgetown's as a model, Dr. Gordon organized her own Symposium for students, administrators, and members of the faculty at Hinds. Although the discussions of Emerson's essays and *King Lear* took place at the Hinds Junior College on October 9, 1986, they are included here because they reflect the spirit of Georgetown's Symposia.

* * *

Other individuals, besides the distinguished speakers, contributed, often with remarkable generosity, to making the two Symposia at Georgetown successful and memorable. Timothy S. Healy, S.J., and J. Donald Freeze, S.J., then President and Provost of the University offered ideas, encouragement, hospitality, and financial support. (Fr. Healy's welcoming remarks at the first Symposium have been made into an introduction to the volume.) Kenneth E. Eble, late Professor of English and University Professor, University of Utah; James R. Kelly, Professor of Sociology, Fordham University; Jo Ann Moran, Associate Professor of History, Georgetown University; and William Richardson, S.J., Professor of Philosophy, Boston College served as respondents for the first symposium. (Fr. Richardson's thoughtful, sensitive reflection on Admiral Stockdale's discussion of Epictetus has been included to suggest the integral contributions these four respondents made to the success of the first Symposium.) Peter F. Krogh, Dean of the School of Foreign Service, and Richard B.

Schwartz, Dean of the Graduate School, participated as speakers. Royden B. Davis, S.J., then Dean of Georgetown College, offered the closing reflections on the first Symposium and introduced one of the speakers at the second. Charles J. Bierne, S.J., then Associate Dean of the School of Business; Bradley B. Billings, Associate Professor of Economics; John B. Breslin, S.J., then Director of the Georgetown University Press; William B. Cooke, Assistant Professor in the School of Business Administration; Joan M. Holmer, Associate Professor of English; Thomas M. King, S.J., Professor of Theology; Anthony T. Moore, Associate Dean of the School for Summer and Continuing Education; Steven R. Sabat, Assistant Professor of Psychology; James V. Schall, S.J., Professor of Government; Annette N. Shelby, Associate Professor in the School of Business Administration; Barbara Stowasser, Associate Professor of Arabic; and George J. Viksnins, Professor of Economics introduced speakers and managed the various sessions of the Symposia. Emma M. Harrington, Ann T. Zuber, and Patricia A. Davis of the School for Summer and Continuing Education provided generous administrative and editorial assistance. Robert A. DiVito, now Assistant Professor of Theology at Loyola University of Chicago, assisted in shaping and managing both Symposia. Charles L. Currie, S.J., the Director of Georgetown's Bicentennial Celebration, helped orchestrate and publicize the second Symposium that opened Georgetown's Bicentennial celebration and provided funds to support the publication of the discussions. To all these men and women, generous friends and colleagues, we are deeply grateful, and we dedicate this book to them.

Georgetown University MICHAEL J. COLLINS
October 8, 1991 FRANCIS J. AMBROSIO

Introduction

What Georgetown did at its Symposia on Text and Teaching was, when you come to think of it, routine. What changed it from the routine were the splendid folk who did it. But essentially a university is really a place of texts, and everybody in the university, all the way down to its youngest members, has his or her favorite. The fun is that we start with young ones and grow, the way I think people move from the Romantics back to Bach. And we acknowledge in the way we grow and the way we change that the factor of time is deeply important for the texts as we find them, but not important for our relation to the texts. And thus, in defiance of chronology, I can record in my own life the obvious movements from *Romeo and Juliet* to *Antony and Cleopatra;* the perhaps less obvious movement from *As You Like It* to *Lear* and *The Sonnets;* and the one that surprised me the most in over twenty years of reading Chaucer, the discovery that I honestly enjoyed "The Knight's Tale" more than "The Miller's."

What we were asking in a very real sense was a university kind of question. What text feeds your soul? And the fun of it was that we found so many interesting fellow citizens to come and tell us, to come and answer that question for us. But in doing that, we posed ourselves a very real problem. There used to be a program on British radio when I was a graduate student (for all I know it may still be there). It was called "Desert Island Discs," and it gathered famous people and asked them, "If you were going to be marooned on a desert island, what records, musical records, would you take with you and why?" And people gave a variety of answers, some of them ludicrous, and some of them very revealing. And then the last question in the program was always, "Aside from the Bible and Shakespeare, what book would you take with you?" The answers to that were really startling sometimes. Gilbert Chesterton answered, "Bright's *Practical Guide to Shipbuilding*."

The answers on "Desert Island Discs" were always puzzling, as indeed were some of the answers at the Symposia. I'll confess to finding a certain logic in Justice Brennan, who was about to begin his thirtieth term on the Supreme Court, focusing on the Constitution. It is, after all, the way he earned his living. But, for an admiral and a hero of a war to come up with Epictetus surprised even the academy.

The problem is, of course, that possession is a two-way street. To paraphrase John Steinbeck, it's living with a book; it's studying it; it's crying into or laughing over it; it's needing it; it's trusting it that sets up possession. Whereas the book can be shared, that process cannot. So the purpose of the Symposia was to chase all of us, the listeners, back to great texts. The mystery each speaker revealed can be repeated, but it cannot be shared.

When English teachers have difficult things to say, they instinctively reach for poets. There is a very beautiful poem by Ted Hughes which I have used in a letter to freshmen, probably much to their mystification, which to me describes to perfection the difficult and very subtle request we made of our speakers and the demand we teachers place on ourselves. It is called "Brooktrout."

> *The Brooktrout, superb as a matador,*
> *Sways invisible there*
> *In water empty as air.*
>
> *The Brooktrout leaps, gorgeous as a jaguar,*
> *But dropping back into swift glass*
> *Resumes clear nothingness.*
>
> *The numb-cold current's brain-wave is lightning—*
> *No good shouting: "Look!"*
> *It vanished as it struck.*
>
> *You can catch Brooktrout, a goggling gewgaw—*
> *But never the flash God made*
> *Drawing the river's blade.*

TIMOTHY S. HEALY, S.J.

Edmund D. Pellegrino, M.D.*

ON

The Book of Job

> How wonderful were your scriptures! How profound! We see their surface and it attracts us like children. And yet, O God, their depth is stupendous. We shudder to peer into them, for they inspire in us both the awe of reverence and the thrill of love.
> St. Augustine, *The Confessions*

I. INTRODUCTION: JOB, THE PARADIGM OF SUFFERING

Literary masterworks survive, not because they resolve some universal human dilemma, but precisely because they do not. Their special appeal lies in the fact that they confront the mystery of human existence; they do so in exalted language that evokes the tremendum of religious experience and they offer multiple levels of interpretation and meaning. They leave the fundamental questions tantalizingly unanswered, but also tantalizingly alive for every era to ponder. All lasting works center on the question of man to which, as Karl Rahner has said, "... there is no answer." Job is preeminently such a book.

Job confronts the enigma of human suffering directly, poignantly and in sublime poetic language. It leaves us deeply disquieted, but never indifferent. Job has been read in a multitude of ways: as a paradigm of patience; a test of righteousness; a proof that good may

---

*Doctor Pellegrino is director of the Kennedy Institute of Ethics and John Carroll Professor of Medicine and Medical Ethics. He is also a member of the Linacre Quarterly editorial advisory board.

come from evil; an evidence of the meaninglessness of human existence; a proof of God's indifference, or His moral ambivalence. Some conclude that the answer to Job's question is abandonment to God's will; others, the rejection of God as a cosmic sadist; and others that human, not divine, love is the only reality upon which we can rely. Whatever the interpretation, all ages have recognized that the Book of Job describes an inescapable human experience, one that each of us ultimately must confront and to which we must fashion a personal response.

Paul Claudel, the French poet-diplomat, after 50 years of struggling with the meaning of the Book of Job, concluded that, "it is the most sublime, the most poignant, the most daring, and at the same time the most disappointing . . . and the most offensive of the books of the Bible." As an enigma, its closest competitor is that other strangely fascinating piece of Wisdom literature, the Book of Ecclesiastes.

Even a partial list of the luminaries who, like Claudel, puzzled over Job's intriguing text, is overwhelming in length and intellectual power. Among the *saints* we find Jerome, Chrysostom and Gregory, the latter devoting four entire books of meditation to Job's dilemma. Among the *theologians* we can count Luther, Kierkegaard, Buber, Danielou, and Calvin. The latter was moved to devote 159 sermons to Job. The *philosophers* include Maimonides, Spinoza, Hobbes, Kant, Nietzsche, Royce, Paul Weiss, and Walter Kaufman. 'The *writers* include Lamartime, Voltaire, D. H. Lawrence, and Robert Frost. Archibald MacLeish cast Job as a modern businessman. William Blake illustrated the Book of Job with his mystical engravings.

If to this partial list, we add all those who have wrestled with the theme of human suffering and its meaning, we would embrace much of the world's great literature—from the folk tales of Ancient Egypt and the Middle East, through Sophocles, Aeschylus, and Euripides, to Marcus Aurelius, St. Augustine, Dante, Shakespeare, and Goethe to Dostoyevski, De Unamuno, Camus, Kafka, John Gardner and Samuel Beckett. No serious writer or thinker has been able to ignore Job's anguish, his questions and his desperate need for answers. Can we believe in God with the mysteries of evil and justice unanswered? Does suffering have meaning? Does meaning itself exist? All art ultimately must touch these questions, or remain forever ephemeral and on the surface of life.

What can a physician add to what has already been so copiously and perceptively written about Job? I am neither an exegete, biblical scholar, philosopher, theologian, or literary critic. I cannot discourse on the metaphysical compatibility of evil with the existence of a good and just God. Nor can I add anything to the learned debates about the provenance, authorship, chronology, unity, linguistics, or poetic merits of the text.

My own fascination with the text of Job is as a paradigm of human suffering—physical and spiritual. As such, it speaks to the physician who meets Job daily in the suffering of his patients. He is under a moral imperative to comprehend that experience as best he can. Without that comprehension the physician cannot fully help or heal. Without it, he cannot prepare for the inevitable experience of his own suffering.

What I can offer is one physician's meditation on Job, on what the text reveals of the nature of suffering, its impact on the human spirit, and the things we must understand to help each other in the presence of illness and misfortune. I shall concentrate on the human experience of Job, his friends' efforts to console him, and the insights we can gain from Job's dialogues with his friends. I will comment on what this rich text reveals to doctors, nurses, patients, and pastoral counselors, and all of us. Job is a text we must study if we are to be healers rather than wounders of the sick and the afflicted.

I know even these aims are not modest. But, at least, I hope to avoid the intellectual and spiritual arrogance of another physician who commented on Job's text. In his *Answer to Job*, the physician-psychologist, Carl Jung, humbly promised to meditate on the text " . . . as a layman, and a physician who had been privileged to see deeply into the psychic depth of many people." Instead of keeping that promise, however, Jung had the audacity to put God on the analytic couch. He found God entrapped in a Manichean emotional conflict, caught between His good and evil natures. God, according to Jung, was guilt-ridden because He violated the Covenant in His treatment of Job. Jung even pictured God as envying Job and projecting His own guilt on him. The Incarnation, on this view, is God's way of reparation for the injustice done Job. On the way to this bizarre conclusion, Jung also psychoanalyzed Christ, Ezekiel, and St. John and reinterpreted the doctrine of the Assumption! Jung achieved a level of hubris unparalleled even in a profession not particularly noted for its humility! While I may not, by the nature of my task, avoid pretentiousness entirely, I think I can avoid Jung's own Super-Jehovah complex.

II. OUTLINE OF THE BOOK

The line of Job's story is of the utmost simplicity. It has what Northrop Frye has called a "U" shape. Job starts out prosperous; he is smitten by calamities; Job is restored to his former status. Within that simple line lies one of the most profound metaphysical and spiritual odysseys in all of literature.

The story of Job was originally probably limited to Chapters 1, 2, and 42, what are now the prologue and epilogue. The intervening poetic portion is a later addition to the "story."

The book of Job opens in heaven where we learn that Job, a prosperous and righteous desert chieftain in the land of Uz, is beloved by God for his piety and faithfulness. Satan is scandalized by such a paragon of virtue and challenges God's trust in Job. Job's piety, Satan says, is nothing but well disguised self-interest. Satan taunts God, "Just reach out and strike what he has, and he will curse you to your face." (1:11)* God is so confident of Job's righteousness that he turns Job over to Satan's power, at first exempting only Job's person from harm.

Job is visited by a series of calamities. He loses all his flocks. His home is destroyed and all his children killed. Yet, Job remains faithful. "Yahweh gave, and Yahweh took away. Blessed be Yahweh's name." (1:21) But Satan is still not satisfied. He challenges God further, "reach out and strike him. Touch his bone and flesh and he will curse you to your face" (2:5). God, still confident of Job's righteousness, hands him over to Satan's power "only spare his life," (2:6) He says to Satan. Job is now afflicted with a terrible skin disease and reduced to a pitiful state, seated on an ash heap, scraping himself with a potsherd. So dismal is his predicament that Job's wife tells him to curse God and die. Job refuses, saying, "Shall we accept good from God and not accept evil?" (2:10)

At this point, the story changes from prose to the most powerful kind of poetry. Job is visited by three friends. At first, when they see the state to which he has fallen, they grieve silently with him for seven days and nights. Job then delivers a soliloquy lamenting his fate, cursing the day of his birth and yearning for death to release him from his sufferings.

His three friends can no longer contain their silence. Each delivers several cycles of speeches to which Job replies. Each speaker sets forth, in various ways, the traditional teaching that evil is the wages of sin. They imply, at first indirectly, and then by direct accusation, that Job or his children have sinned in some way or they would not

---

*All quotations from the *Anchor Bible*, translated by Marvin Pope (see references).

be punished by a just and good God. Job vehemently denies their accusations and vigorously protests his friends' rationalizations. He refuses to confess to transgressions he has not committed. Job challenges God's righteousness. He prays fervently for someone to hear his case—some neutral judge—whom he can confront face-to-face. If only he could present his case, the injustice of his sufferings would be clear.

Job's debate with his friends ends in stalemate and Job soliloquizes again, protesting his innocence. He recites the code of righteous behavior by which he has lived his whole life. He pleads again for God to answer him. Now a new counselor, named Elihu, enters the debate. He is a young and arrogant man who castigates Job's three friends for their ineffectiveness in arguing with Job. He launches into his own long tirade against Job's protestations of innocence—using the same arguments as the others, but more vehemently and more accusingly.

Finally, God does speak directly to Job, out of a whirlwind. He does not answer Job in Job's terms. Instead, in magnificent verse, He hurls a series of ironic questions at Job. God questions Job's fitness to understand even the simplest mysteries of His creation. Yet these, wondrous as they are, are far from exhausting God's power. Job is mistaken to think that God or the moral order of His universe, can be understood in human terms or measured by man. God challenges Job, "will the contender with Shaddai yield? He who reproves God, let him answer for it." (40:2).

Job is overwhelmed. He has had the confrontation he begged for, but not as he could possibly have imagined. Job admits he is of small account, "Lo I am small, how can I answer you?" (40:4), and resolves to speak no more. But the Lord continues His challenges. Would Job dare to condemn God, that he might justify himself? (40:8) God continues His rhapsody on the mysteries of the cosmos which man cannot understand, including the existence of evil. At no point does the Lord use any of the conventional explanations so laboriously and confidently argued by Job's friends.

Job has now had his wish. He has seen the Almighty with his own eyes. He abases himself before God and repents for the folly of daring to be God's critic. He no longer asks for reason, but for compassion: "I had heard of you by hearsay, but now my eyes have seen you. So, I recant and repent in dust and ashes." (42:5-6) The book ends in a prose epilogue in which God chastises Eliphaz, one of Job's friends: "My anger burns against you and your two friends for you have not spoken the truth of me as Job did." (42:7-8)

Job's friends must offer sacrifice, but they will not be forgiven unless Job prays for them. Job's prosperity is restored several-fold; his honor is regained, he lives a long life, and dies in peace.

III. THE ODYSSEY OF JOB'S SUFFERING

In his preface to *Prometheus Unbound*, Shelley warns about the non-transposability of prose and poetry and his abhorrence for didacticism in poetry. All attempts to extract explicit meanings or morals from poetry as exalted as Job's run the risk of puerility. It is what Job's poetry evokes in each of us about the human experience of suffering that draws us irresistibly. We can see Job in ourselves, our families, friends, and our patients. In Job's dialogue with his friends, we recognize our own attempts to help and to give some rational grounding to suffering. We feel Job's anger, protestations, and puzzlement, his sense of injustice and alienation. Everywhere they greet us: in every hospital, home for the aged and retarded, in the hospices, the prisons, in the victims of the holocaust, and in every oppressed land. The sheer massiveness of human misery and the inevitability that we, too, will suffer, hover silently over even the most prosperous of us.

The physician sees all of this up close in the inhabitants of that city of suffering—the hospital he traverses daily. He sees how illness shocks, shatters, and estranges. He cannot help being pulled into the sufferer's experience if he is truly a healer and not simply a tinker of diseased organs and disabled bodies. To be sure, the physician must practice detachment—but he must practice a compassionate detachment. He must have a capacity to step back from Job's ills and anguish, to diagnose them accurately so as to treat them rationally. But, if he is also to help, he must confront, with his patients, the deeper anguish that transcends the pain and the physical ravages of the disease.

Illness and sickness create the deepest suffering and the most severe test of life's meaning. Recall that neither God nor Satan regarded Job as fully tested until his "flesh and bone" were touched. Job suffered the loss of all he cherished. While Job lamented his losses loudly and pitifully, he sank into the deepest depths of his despair and resentment only when God permitted Satan to afflict him with a frightful skin disease. It is after this that Job began to hurl his sharpest blasphemies, questions, accusations, and bitterness at God.

Once personal illness is added to Job's other burdens, he is like the Psalmist "on the brink of Sheol," "a man bereft of strength."

(Psalm 88)* He oscillates between abjectly begging for the death and pleading for restoration of his health. He accuses the very God from Whom he demands justice. Over and over again, Job asks, as does every afflicted human. Why? Why me? Why now? Why not all the unrighteous who prosper and live long lives? "What have I done to you, man watcher? Why have you made me your target? Why am I a burden to you?" (7:20) But Job gets no answer, even after he confronts God eye-to-eye. The mystery of suffering must remain a mystery; it is beyond human rationality. Job learns that no human has a claim on God. No human can presume to be a critic of the cosmic order. Job is finally overwhelmed and reconciled, not by a reasonable explanation, but by a religious experience. He is struck by awe and fear of the Lord and painfully learns the lesson of the psalmist of Psalm 111, or in Job's own words: "Behold the fear of the Lord, that is wisdom. To turn from evil is understanding." (28:28)

For the physician, Job is the incarnation of his own patient with whom the physician goes through the experience of suffering. Illness is a special assault on the whole person—as much on the spirit as on the body. Suffering is more than physiological pain. Pain and painless disease, alike, beget anguish because they contract the possibilities of human existence. The horizons of what may be hoped for are foreshortened. The afflicted is, in Job's words, one ". . . whose way is hidden, whom God has fenced about." (3:23) Sickness is the unfailing evidence of our ultimate and ineradicable finitude—the sign of the fragility of personal existence. It exposes unequivocally the vulnerability, dependence, expendability, and exploitability always lurking just beneath the surface of human life. It terrifies the one who is ill, and those who attend him or are dear to him.

The one who is sick can no longer define and pursue his own goals. The purposes of his life are predetermined by the disease. It takes center-stage. Sickness makes the body and the mind the enemy of the self; it obtunds all plans. It forces a confrontation with the numinous: "Why do you rear man at all? Or pay any mind to him? Inspect him every morning? Test him every moment?" (7:17-18) How shall I respond, what shall I say, how shall I live? The answers must be our own if we are to remain persons. Men and women can endure extreme pain and suffering when there is hope, or explanation. Without these, the suffering person faces the terrible possibility of a dissolution of his entire being.

---

*Text of the Jerusalem Bible

Suffering demands that endurance and dying be personal enterprises. It unmercifully exposes our freedom to fashion a personal response. In that freedom lies the paradoxical possibility of healing even the dying patient. Unlike Job, we must respond without seeing God eye-to-eye, without directly confronting His ineffability. To embrace or reject suffering, to make it our own experience and not become its passive object, is the final test of that autonomy we hold so dear when we are healthy.

WIDE RANGE OF RESPONSES

Physicians, families, and friends must be prepared for a wide, unpredictable and often shocking range of responses to Job's questions posed by the sick person they love, and think they know. Is suffering a punishment for sin, or is it a preventive? Is it a means of atonement and reconciliation? Or is it, as the Stoics said, an inexorable, inexplicable law of nature, useless to resist? Is suffering evidence, as some Existentialists would have it, of God's indifference or the meaninglessness of meaning itself? Is it the way of salvation as Christ taught? Or is it, as Nietzsche insisted, that the whole idea of salvation itself is the result of the Christian's "inability to let suffering be senseless." Is the sufferer, like Kafka's protagonist, accused of an unspecified crime by an accuser he will never meet? Is he, like Oedipus, suffering because of a curse on his family, or like Prometheus, for opposing God's will, like Lear or MacBeth, for a defect of character, or like Jason and Medea, for an excess of hubris?

The whole complex, contradictory and vacillating nexus of rationalizations of suffering is incarnated in each sick and suffering human. And it is into this tangled nexus that the physician and others must enter. In the modern world, suffering is not very often accepted, simply and submissively, as God's will, as Job first accepted it. Rather, modern man resists openly the affront to pride and self-esteem, which misfortune, disease, and death represent. Job himself was not entirely the model of steadfast faith and patience which St. James makes him out to be. (5:11)

Job's text teaches us how to discern the many ways in which humans react to suffering. We must comprehend the range of those responses if we are to help, and not exacerbate the suffering. Despite Shelley's abhorrence for the didactic, we must yet look at the more mundane practical lessons Job's human predicament can teach all of us.

We note, for example, that Job's friends spent a week with him in silence. Considering their later clumsy attempts to console him, this was perhaps the best thing they did. Their presence was a genuine act of empathy. It is the first step we, too, must take—to *be* with the sick, to listen to their soliloquies, to say just enough to show we are there, and to allow their hurt to show itself. A receptive silence, one that communicates compassionate concern without pitying, allows the patient to vent his resentment and anger to another person.

But, like Job, the patient is, in reality, speaking to God. There is, in us, a deep impulse to vent our sufferings. We who attend the sick are privileged witnesses to those struggles. The sick person sooner or later knows that there may be no answer to his questions. What he needs is our understanding that the struggle is a personal, deeply spiritual and perilous one. Often we help most if we help least—if we listen in silence, as Job's friends did at first.

Like them, we cannot remain forever silent. Inevitably we must enter the experiences of illness and suffering in *this* person. But we must do so without shock, surprise, or moralizing. We must not allow our sensibilities to be offended by what we hear in the patient's soliliquy. Above all, we must avoid trying to win an argument: "But what does your arguing prove?" (6:25) Like Job's counselors, in our zeal for explanation we run the risk of becoming not friends, but accusers, usurping God's prerogatives of judgment.

We cannot rightfully expect that God will speak directly to us as He did to Job. Yet we must not forget that Job himself, even before he had his confrontation with God, knew that he could not win his case against God. "But how can man be acquitted before God? If He deigned to litigate with him, could he answer Him one in a thousand?" (9:2-3) "He is not like me, a man I could challenge, 'Let us go to court together.'" (9:32) The inescapable fact is that Job cannot argue his case against God nor can Job's friends presume to argue God's case against Job.

Most offensive to Job, and to any suffering or sick person, are condescension and presumption. Let us listen to Job's own words to his friends:

> I know as much as you know
> I am not inferior to you
> Rather would I speak with Shaddai
> I wish to remonstrate with God
> But you are daubers of deceit,
> Quack healers all of you

> I wish you would keep strictly silent
> That would be wisdom in you. (13:2-5)

We need to appreciate, too, that the experience of illness is not penetrable by others and none of us can know how we will respond. Thus, Job says to his friends:

> Will it be well when he probes you?
> Can you trick him as men are tricked? (13:9)

> Will not his fear overwhelm you? (13:11)

> Your maxims are ashen aphorisms
> Defenses of clay your defenses.
> Be silent before me that I may speak. (13:12-13)

God Himself agreed with Job and castigated Job's friends just as severely for not speaking truly. He preferred Job's honest protestations to the pious hypocrisy of his friends who dared to argue God's case against Job. If we are to avoid the same condemnation, we must listen carefully to Job's words when we are in the presence of our suffering patients, families, or friends.

Job, like his counterparts in every age, asks repeatedly for our compassionate listening, not moralizing speeches:

> Pity me, Pity me, Oh my friends.
> For the hand of God has struck me.
> Why do you pursue me like God? (19:21-22)

> Hear my word attentively,
> Let this be the solace you give.
> Bear with me, let me speak,
> When I have spoken, mock on. (21:2-3)

Over and over again, Job beseeches his friends to hear him out, to understand his plight, to feel compassion for his predicament, but not to preach to him.

In some of the most forceful words in all literature, Job speaks for all the suffering in all the ages. We are all tempted to play the roles of Bildad, Zophar and Eliphaz, and some of us, even the more arrogant role of Elihu. Job is blunt in his condemnation of their theologizing. He speaks eloquently for all those patient sufferers who, out of deference, do not tell us to "shut up" as Job so forthrightly told his friends.

We must be prepared, therefore, if we would help, to hear outpourings of rage, doubt, uncertainty, despair, hope and numbness all intermingled. They will come from believers and non-believers alike.

So estimable a Christian as C. S. Lewis, in the depth of his own grief at the loss of his wife, went so far as to say:

> The conclusion I dread is not 'So there's no God after all' but 'so this is what God's really like. Deceive yourself no longer.' How often had bitter resentment been stifled through sheer terror, and an act of love—in every sense an act—put on to hide the operation? (Lewis went even further:) Is it rational to believe in a bad God? Any way in a God so bad as all that? The cosmic sadist?

We are shocked by such language, coming as it does from a committed Christian. Remember that C. S. Lewis, before his own grief, wrote one of the most coherent and rational treatises on the metaphysical and theological problem of evil. Even so fine an intellect could be crushed by the actual presence of suffering.

But Lewis's odyssey, like Job's, finally led him to reconciliation: "and so, with God, I have gradually been coming to feel that the door is no longer shut and bolted. Was it my own frantic need that slammed it in my face?" We who would help must be humble before such anguished cries. We must stay with the sufferer as he descends the limb of his despair and his hurt. We must hope, and pray, and listen, as he struggles to reascend the other limb of the same "U" that Job traversed. We presume too much if we think our logic can give meaning to suffering before the sick man, like Job, has met God in the crucible of his suffering. Meaning does not come from syllogisms.

We must remember again and again, that God chastised Job's friends for their pietistic formulae. God suffered Job's sharp rebukes. God alone understood the full depths of Job's anguish. We cannot forget that Christ Himself in those last moments of His own anguish, uttered those forever chilling words:

> When the sixth hour came, there was darkness over all the earth until the ninth hour; and at the ninth hour, Jesus cried out with a loud voice, 'My God, My God, why has thou forsaken me?'
> (Mark 15:35)

Even Christ, Who knew the Father and His purposes, felt the human experience of abandonment in His darkest hour of suffering.

Job reminds us, too, that we cannot fully comprehend another's suffering. We cannot hope to understand why *this* person responds *this* way. It is too easy when we are well to preach and criticize:

> I have heard plenty of this;
> Galling comforters are you all

> Have windy words no limit?
> What moves you to prattle on?
> I, too, could talk like you.
> If you were in my place.
> I could harangue you with words,
> Could shake my head at you. (16:2-4)

Pierre Wolff, in an arresting but profound little book entitled, *May I Hate God?*, probes the depths of feelings we may expect from those who suffer. He warns that hatred can overcome reason but that hate is itself a sign of residual love. We cannot hate that to which we are indifferent. Job's friends accuse him of blasphemy. But as Wolff points out, behind Job's seeming blasphemy there was more love than in the sterile, hypocritical piety of Job's friends. Indifference is a form of murder, because it erases a person from our consciousness. Indifference is what most wounds the sick in today's hospitals at the hands of competent but detached health professionals.

Job was not indifferent to God as a Stoic or existentialist might be. Nor was God indifferent to Job. He confronted Job eye-to-eye. He thundered at him. He did so because in Job's anger He detected love. And for his part, Job detected God's love for him even while he had to learn the impossibility of ever fully understanding evil.

ABIDE COMPLAINTS, RESENTMENTS

We must abide the sufferer's complaints and resentments because the need to express them is a cry for help. All health professionals have an obligation to help the sick person to express these feelings in his own way. This is the first step toward healing the wounded humanity of the sufferer. Somehow we must help him heal his relationship with God, the cosmos, and his own humanity. Allowing the sufferer to reveal the content of his suffering is to respect his dignity as a person. It is one way to negate the alienation from the human community which the sick person so desperately feels.

Whoever opens himself to the revelations of the inner self of another assumes moral obligations. Too often, the patient stifles his anguish for fear of ridicule and rejection. We must never belittle the sentiments of the sick, or take advantage of their vulnerability. To use that vulnerability to convert, or to proselytize, is to usurp the place of God with Whom the only meaningful confrontation can occur. That is what Job's friends did, to the disgust of both God and Job.

This does not mean that we must be altogether mute, that we are not to offer spiritual consolation, or help the sufferer find meanings in his sufferings. We can respond to his probings, share our own faith and convictions and our own questionings and prayers with him. What he needs most is our compassion—a conviction that we genuinely feel something of his predicament, that we understand its uniqueness and impenetrability. This impenetrability does not dissolve the common bond of humanity between us. It is this bond that ties us to all suffering humankind.

If we, too, have suffered affliction, we must beware of using the sick person as an excuse to exhibit it, to impress him with our experience, or to assuage our own anguish. Some of the more zealous organized efforts to help others to "deal with" their grief can trample on the uniqueness and privacy of the experience. There is no "approved" way to suffer, grieve or die. But whatever way fits the patient, he can be helped if we listen, meditate his questions with him, avoid reproach, and avoid trying to win a debate.

Some of the sufferer's troubles will be self-generated to be sure: the result of his own acts or attitudes to suffering itself. Nonetheless, we do best if we hear out the patient's lament and absorb some of his hostility and resentment. To do so is not to praise or agree with it. This is a bogus brand of compassion, cheaply bought and cheaply given, more suited to mutual self-satisfaction than genuinely helping.

Often the patient has a profound need to lash out in frustration at someone or something. Often, it is those nearby—the doctor, nurse, or family—on whom the hostility is displaced. C. S. Lewis put it this way:

> All that stuff about the cosmic sadist is not so much an expression of thought as of hatred. I was getting the only pleasure a man in anguish can get, the pleasure of hitting back.

Physicians and others who receive these lashings must understand their origin, must absorb some of the hostility, and must not strike back. To strike back, or to avoid the patient is to neglect a prime moral imperative of the professional healer.

Many of the complaints we hear today about the aloofness, inhumaneness, and indifference of modern medicine arise from the neglect by physicians and nurses of the vivid lessons Job teaches. Much of the current emphasis on "humanism" in medical education derives from a need to inculcate some measure of compassion in the physician's education. Without compassion, the physician's competence can be damaging or simply self-serving. Job's text is an indispensable *vade mecum* for those who presume to help and heal the sick and the suffering.

We can speak of healing even if the patient is beyond our help scientifically. Reflecting on Job's experience, it was not death he feared so much as abandonment, the injustice he saw in his afflictions, the lack of a chance to make his case heard, to confront his God, to be able to abjure the indifference of the cosmos to his plight. Limited as our powers may be, the true healer is committed to helping the patient to reassemble his life to the extent possible even in fatal illness. We may not be able to reexpand the contracted horizon of possibilities, but we can help the afflicted person make his own response in his own way, and, thus, restore some of the wholeness of his person lost in the assault of illness.

For those who have a religious faith, hope can be restored, not necessarily in recovery, but in reassembling some meaning to life that lies in the possibilities of a personal response to suffering. Even in naturalistic terms, suffering is not without value to the sufferer and those around him. No one has understood this better than Miguel de Unamuno. Only a few quotes from his *Tragic Sense of Life* will suffice:

> Suffering is the substance of life and the root of personality for only suffering makes us persons. (224)

> Suffering is a spiritual matter and the most immediate revelation of consciousness, and it may be that our body was not given to us except as a means of suffering. Whoever has never suffered much or little has no consciousness of himself. (231)

> For in truth, human beings love each other spiritually only when they have suffered the same sorrow, when they have ploughed the stony earth joined together by the mutual yoke of a common grief. It is then that they know one another and feel for and feel with one another in their common anguish and pity one another and love one another. (149)

Miguel de Unamuno's profound insights into human suffering reveal the possibilities of personal growth inherent in anguish. His observations are first steps to the deeper understanding that comes from religious faith. I have not attempted to deal at this level because others have done so eloquently. I have confined myself to a meditation as a physician. But as a believing Roman Catholic Christian, I see the existential predicament of the suffering human, as Job did, as primarily a spiritual and religious experience. Pope John Paul II, in his beautiful apostolic letter, *On Human Suffering*, has summarized what the Christian faith teaches about suffering and healing to those who profess it.

Job's text can be read on many levels. Only one has occupied me here: the text's sublime evocation of one human being's encounter with the most universal experience of all—suffering and illness. No matter what progress medicine may make, how long it may extend our lives, or how carefree our existence may become, the experience of suffering will remain, and will not deviate much from Job's account.

Job's text will always inspire, instruct, and intrigue every age to come. For the physician and the nurse, it is an indispensable textbook. But it is a book for all of us, especially today when we equate the experiences of illness and healing with a commodity transaction or an experiment in applied biology, or the fixing of a piece of machinery or an opportunity for medical entrepreneurship. Suffering and illness are extravagant contradictions to our Promethean aspirations. We see those who succumb to them as a scandal. So we sequester them in hospitals and nursing homes; we complain about how much they cost us and how much they demand of our time and energy. We urge them to die sooner, or we deny them life entirely when they are malformed before or after birth.

Our age needs to ponder the Book of Job so as to regain its bearings, to understand that the sick and suffering have a moral claim on us. For the doctor and nurse, Job remains the text par excellence which teaches what suffering is about. For the rest of us, it is the reminder of the confrontation we cannot escape, the confrontation which paradoxically, as Unamuno said, ". . . is the substance of life and the root of personality for only suffering makes us persons."

Job is, and will remain, the book we must all eventually live. It comes as close as any book to what Carlyle called it, "the greatest book ever written with pen." But the Book of Job is part of a greater book—the book which transcends literature and aesthetics and whose "very nature" it is to "affront, perplex, and astonish the human mind." (Merton 1)

Job is one of the oldest parts of the Bible. Early on, God issued His powerful challenge to our demands for justice. Centuries later, He challenged us again. Paul Claudel puts it this way:

> We have reached Gethsemane. This is not the story of a rich proprietor's loss of his estates, of a family's loss of its children and of bone and flesh being seized upon by a blind and ignorant enemy. This is Gethsemane, where God was made man. God took

upon Himself all the horror of mankind. Behold old Job! You asked for Justice and here He is in answer to your plea. You asked Him to appear as an equal. He has done that. What have you to say? (Claudel 9)

For some of us, this is the answer to Job's and our own odyssey through anguish to the fulfillment prophesied by Isaiah, "He was bruised for our iniquities and the chastisement of our peace was upon him and with his stripes we are healed." (53:5)

For others, the mystery remains. The magnificence of Job is not that we can question it for answers, but that it questions us, and poses the right question. For the physician, Job is his patient and himself. Sickness is the event that forces the question upon modern man. How will we respond? How will we help others, and ourselves, when the inevitable overtakes us?

WILLIAM J. BENNETT

ON

Plato's Republic

If I understand my task correctly this morning, it is not to confront Plato's theory of justice as developed in *The Republic*, to lay out the argument for justice as presented specifically in Books I and II and developed later on. Rather, my task, as I understand it, is to engage an account of a different sort of confrontation, specifically, the confrontation of a young student in 1961 with the first two books of *The Republic* and some thorny and fundamental questions about justice—how this confrontation occurred, why it occurred, and why it might bear repeating.

The task, then, is somewhat autobiographical, an intellectual autobiography, but I take it as more involved than that. First, then, the facts—the relevant historical facts and some personal facts. The setting for Books I and II of *The Republic* in my life: the first setting was in 1961, the fall, when I was a freshman at Williams College. My interest in philosophy as a freshman at Williams was slight at best. I was a prodigious reader and had been through high school. In fact, I had developed my interest in reading at home in grammar school in Brooklyn and then had been asked to read a lot, and read a lot on my own in high school here in Washington, D.C. So although I had read a great deal, I did not regard myself, and I don't think I could have fairly been regarded as precocious, certainly not as an intellectual. And the thing that is clearest in my memory arriving at Williams, was that I was not intellectually sophisticated. Now, my notion of sophistication at 18 was not altogether full or accurate. Nevertheless, one forms impressions about these things at such an age, so let me tell you the impressions that I was forming. When I first got to Williams, a series of events the first few days made me question whether I should be there. I had, in fact, asked the headmaster at my high school, Gonzaga, where he had wanted me to go. It was not unusual in that day to ask the headmaster where he wanted you to go. I said, "Is it Georgetown or Holy Cross or B.C.?" Those were the usual options at the time. He said, "No, I want to you go someplace like Williams or Dartmouth or Harvard. You are in a contrary pose, and I want you being contrary there." So off I went. The first memory of Williams is arriving at the freshman dormitories, looking at the freshman quad, and seeing something I had never seen before in my life—a lacrosse stick. Williams has a lot of people from private schools, prep schools, and a lot of them played lacrosse. I had seen a basketball, I had seen a football, I had seen a baseball, but I never had seen a lacrosse stick and marvelled at it. That was one. Two, the second day I was there, I was down in the common washroom in Sage Hall where everybody went to brush their teeth, and while I was there, two other freshman came in. And while I was brushing my teeth, I overheard their conversation and I will never forget it. One turned to the other and said, "Brandon"—I had never heard of anyone called Brandon. Everyone I knew was named Steve or Mike or Chris. "Brandon"—this is the honest to God's truth—"Do you realize that the French spoken in Tunis is different from the French spoken in Algiers?" I finished brushing my teeth, I went upstairs, I called my mother, and I said I don't think I belong here, and she said give it a couple of weeks.

On the fourth or fifth day, we had meetings in our halls. We had a system of junior advisors. Junior advisors at the college were there to proctor us, to keep an eye on us freshman. But in the first week we were there, all of the freshmen in the particular dorm unit had discussions led by our proctors about books we had been assigned to read over the summer in preparation. The three were: a book on history and historiography; one on science and human values—Bronowsky, I think, and *The Lord of the Flies*. Well, the conversation soon went to *Lord of the Flies*, which is the book that everybody was the most interested in. I read it, I thought I understood it, and was ready to talk, when a man later to become a close friend—at that time a very precocious 18-year-old freshman—said, "The thing that struck me about his book was its Weltanschauung." At that point, I knew I'd really had it. I'd had good college boards. I'd thought I'd had a very good education, five years of Latin and all, but we'd never had Weltanschauung and all these other things. So, the context here is a bit of intellectual intimidation, and an interest in being as "sophisticated" as many around me.

Now, I said my interest in philosophy was slight. I took the course because there were distribution requirements. If there had not been such distribution requirements, I don't think I would have taken the course. That's important, at least that's very important to me. I'd heard that the Introduction to Philosophy course was pretty good. I wanted to major in English; I loved literature. I wanted to go into advertising and make a lot of money and use the four years at Williams, it was gradually dawning on me, to become sophisticated and to stop being square.

It's important to talk about the teacher of that course, Professor Laszlo Vercennji, a Plato scholar and a man who by then had introduced generations of students at the college to Plato's thought. He is still doing it, and when I saw him two years ago, he looked exactly the same. I think he's wearing the same tweed sport coat, an additional patch on the elbow.

The first assignment in the course was Books I and II of *The Republic*, the first arguments for the first two days. Books I and II of *The Republic* are about justice and, as you know, many opinions are sampled. Cephalos is the first to appear on the stage. He's a good man, old man, a tired manufacturer. He says to Socrates, "Justice is to tell the truth and to pay back what is owed." He moves off the scene pretty quickly. Polemarchos comes in, a younger man. He says, quoting the poet, "Justice is to help your friends and to harm your enemies." And so it began, so we started the discussion.

Again, I have to make mention of the teacher and the text. I think it's William Arrowsmith who says of the great teachers he remembers, that he cannot recall with precision where the texts leave off and the teacher begins. They seem to be one thing. Teacher and text in one combined assault on a young sensibility. As great teachers become so much a part of the text, it was hard for us then, in 1961, to tell what was text and what was teacher. So it was with Professor Vercennji. We have all heard endless, and sometimes painful, accounts of the Socratic technique, but at that time, and in that place, it did seem to me, and to many of my fellow students, as if we were being confronted by a reincarnation of Socrates himself. The topic was justice, and although there were questions about the account given by Polemarchos, Cephalos et al., what began to become clear was that the real question before us was whether this matter of justice was truly a matter for us to take seriously. I can't tell you exactly why, but I think it had something to do with a degree of arrogance about us, with aspirations to cosmopolitanism and a little bit of cynicism, but whatever the reason, I and many of my classmates resisted the notion that this question of justice should be taken seriously. We resisted Socrates and we resisted Vercennji. So we paid more than passing attention to the seriousness of the questions posed to Socrates by the two young men, Glaucon and Adeimantus. Why should a man be just if he can get away with being unjust? We were willing to pose the question, and, indeed, we were willing—sometimes more than willing—to take the opposite side. Most of us were, for whatever reason, closer to the spirit of Thrasymachus, arguing as devil's advocates on his side, half as a challenge to our teacher and, of course, through our teacher, to Socrates.

What was our challenge? It was something like this, I think, that the issue of justice and taking justice seriously was a sham and that this was a kind of fairy tale. We had been taught this before in grade school and high school, but now we were sophisticated people who didn't need to have this told to us anymore. We didn't have to be taught and didn't want to be taught about virtue, political right and wrong. We wanted to be on our way. These were tales told to frighten children into some kind of notion of orderly behavior. We didn't need that. As I said, for whatever reason, we sided with Thrasymachus when he says, "What I say is that what is just or right means nothing but what is in the interest of the stronger party." That, at least, attracted us as the argument we wished to defend.

Now, I suppose our posture here was not so unique, and it certainly has been seen before and since—certainly seen before by the evidence offered by the first two books of *The Republic* itself. My friends who are teachers of philosophy say that it has been seen since, as well. We offered a certain degree of resistance in confronting the theme of justice, just as some of us were interested in offering resistance to other great questions being raised in other classes, questions about courage, or friendship, or power, or valor, or hope, or love, or faith. Socrates asked the young men of Athens, is this a serious pursuit or not? Let's tell the truth, no more fairy tales. Alright, we young men of Williams said, we are not impressed, at least at this point, and do not see why we should take it seriously. Could he hear us saying silently "show us how and why we should take it seriously?" We wanted to get our course work done, we said, get our jobs, and go out and be about our business of getting ahead. Graduates of Williams do a lot of good in the world. Alumni reports suggest that graduates of Williams not only do a lot of good, they do well. But why, again, did we have to get involved in the question? Why was that so important to us? Were we, perhaps, somehow persuading ourselves that we had a vested interest in Thrasymachus being right and agreeing with him when he said a little later on, "Innocent as you are yourself, Socrates, you must see that a just man always has the worst of it and that injustice on a grand enough scale, if the man can get away with it, is superior to justice."

Now, were we interested in injustice for its own sake? No, I don't think that would be accurate. It was rather, I think, that this insistence that we take the question of justice seriously constituted a distraction from our other pursuits, from our theory of a college education. So when I was confronted directly in this argument, I took the side of Thrasymachus. I wanted to win the argument. For these reasons, and also because of some degree of excessive pride, not wanting to be shown up in front of my classmates, we took the argument seriously on the side of Thrasymachus. Many of us really did want to be persuaded that we were wrong, but we weren't going to fall easily. Like Thrasymachus, we were going to put up the best resistance we could. I think it fair to say that for some of us we did want to take the question of justice seriously, but what was very important at that time for 18-year-old young men was that if we did take it seriously, we not be thought of as fools for doing so. We wanted to be convinced, we wanted good reasons for it. The last thing we wanted to do was to appear to be sentimental or square. Remember square?

So the dialogue commences among all of us and the challenges are issued. The arguments took place and went forward tracking Books I and II. It is an article, I think, of agreement among many scholars of Plato that something happens to the participants in the Platonic dialogue, that they walk away not only with their minds changed, but with something else changed, as well. Their opinions are changed, yes, but their insides are shaken up a little bit, too. So we fought our way through it, half the semester on Books I and II. Later, as a teacher of *The Republic*, I rarely, if ever, got past Books I and II with my students; Is it the responsibility of the governor or ruler to pursue his own interest, or is he to pursue the interest of those in whose trust he serves? What does it profit a man to be interested in justice? What if he pursues it, but has his eyes put out and is shamed and falsely accused for doing so? And what about the ring of Gyges? I will never forget the ring of Gyges. If a man had a ring, and with it could make himself invisible, steal around at night, and have everything he wanted, without any worry of being caught, would there be any reason for him to act justly rather than unjustly? Well, most of you know much of the rest of the story. Back and forth, up and down the campus, I argued with Vercennji. To and from class, before class and after class, I called him at home at night with an argument I hadn't thought of in class. He took the call patiently. I argued with classmates and with anyone else, and when I got home I argued with my mother and my brother who could have cared less about Books I and II of *The Republic*, but were glad to see that I was taking it seriously. I was late for football practice a couple of times because of arguments going on in the student union. Not the best arguments, arguments that by Vercennji's light, and I think by the light of many scholars, would not have been regarded as particularly rigorous but impassioned and serious, trying to find our way though it. I remember rehearsing several foolproof refutations before class, going in and being frustrated and embarrassed as my refutation was refuted. Some of us kept demanding over and over again, putting up any argument we possibly could, questioning why the devil was moral excellence, *areté*, man's distinctive excellence? Couldn't you get there another way?

So, that's really the story. I pay tribute to Vercennji and Socrates because they succeeded at least in persuading me, and I know many others, that the question of justice was, indeed, real and that we were not fools for thinking it real. So, I decided to major in philosophy. I later went on to get my Ph.D. and taught philosophy. I will, I hope, teach philosophy again some day. Let me just comment, by way of another reflection based on what happened that freshman year, about going on to graduate school, because one hears and reads a good deal today about graduate work in the humanities and other subjects. What are the job prospects? What are the career opportunities and what are the demographics and the like? Going to graduate school for me and for 16 others in that class had nothing to do with thinking about the job opportunities. There wasn't any career planning in it at all. It was almost as if, once caught up in the enterprise, there was no choice. The question had been raised, some of us had been lured into it, and we were now caught. Vercennji and other teachers committed to raising serious questions with young persons had taken many of us. These men and women and their texts took us. They took us like lovers and we were theirs. So the next three and a half years of my college career were spent principally in involvement with these questions and others like them. In class, out of class, in the fraternity house, at the student union, and a lot of it in faculty offices where the faculty actually were.

I have adjusted and changed my thinking some on politics and political philosophy, and I do not think that *The Republic* is as great a statement about political philosophy and the organization of society as I once thought it was. It is still great and one of the greatest, better on the side of political philosophy than on the side of the organization of society. I think *The Federalist Papers* are an improvement, in part due to the happy circumstance that they could be written 2,000 years later. I should say, however, that when I started to teach, and when, as I plan, I go back to teaching, the focus was and will be again the teaching of ethics and political philosophy. It will be a whole range of books. It will be a whole range of ideas, and it will probably be, when I return to teaching, lots of articles from contemporary magazines, but in some sense it will always be the questions raised in Books I and II of *The Republic*. For it will always be that moment that remains central, that point of entry for me into this whole business; that confrontation of those young men with Socrates on one of the fundamental questions, and our confrontation, our imitation, our replication together with them of what goes on in the dialogue itself. It will always be that that comes to mind when I think about texts and teaching and excellence.

Nancy Landon Kassebaum

ON

Sophocles' Antigone

It is a real honor for me to participate in this symposium as part of the Georgetown University Bicentennial activities. Georgetown has a long history in which it can take enormous pride. Through the years, Georgetown has been the epitome of quality education. The university has provided an environment in which learning is valued and excellence is maintained.

Georgetown students are admonished, in the words of the ancient Greeks, to attain wisdom. Before they leave the campus, they fully understand that wisdom rests not in what we know but in our willingness to learn. This love of learning and willingness to keep learning are legacies which Georgetown has left to generations of scholars.

When I was asked to join in this symposium, I decided first that the theme I most wanted to address was the question of balance and moderation in political life. I did not have a particular text in mind. However, in rereading a favorite book by a favorite author, *Reflections from the North Country* by Sigurd Olson, I was drawn back to the ancient Greeks and specifically to Sophocles and the great tragedy played out in *Antigone*.

Antigone is about balance and order, the necessity of compromise and, ultimately, about the critical capacity to learn. It is about all of the misjudgments, the tragedies, that flow from an unwillingness constantly to see the world through new eyes.

At the end of the play, Creon has destroyed his opposition and, in the process, his family and himself. It is then, and only then, that he utters what must be among the most tormented words of Western civilization:

O how impoverished my deliberations were!

One can only wonder how many times through the intervening centuries other great leaders have been forced, finally, to bow their heads and repeat the painful cry of Creon. Indeed, I believe Creon's lament resonates profoundly in the events of our twentieth century world. We continue to play out the tragic conflicts that Sophocles brought to consciousness so long ago.

We still face Antigone's choice between the conflicting demands of the private person and the public citizen. Isn't that choice a very powerful part of our deliberations over issues such as abortion, gun control, the homeless—or apartheid in South Africa?

We constantly face the struggle between Antigone and Creon as we try to balance the need of the state, the good of all citizens, against the rights of the individual.

At the most basic personal level, each of us confronts the dilemma of Creon, and all his flaws, as we choose either to be enlightened actors in our own life drama or angry victims blinded to the demands of justice by injustices we ourselves have suffered.

Obviously, *Antigone* is rich in material that is both relevant to our time and to our own deliberations as individuals and as a society. For my own purposes here, I want to focus on two questions that relate first to our personal view of the world and then to the institutions we create to balance and blend our individual views into shared consensus and commitment.

I offer these reflections purely as a twentieth century American. I am no expert on either ancient Greek society or classical tragedy. I am certain many others here know more about such things than I do and so, in a sincere way, I am here to learn and not to teach.

Let me begin with a brief summary of *Antigone*'s plot. The two sons of Oedipus have fought for control of Thebes. True to their dead father's curse, they kill each other in battle. Their uncle, Creon, then decrees, as ruler of Thebes, that one will receive the city's full honor in burial as a defender of the city. He orders that the other, the traitorous Polyneices, shall be left on the battlefield and that anyone attempting to bury him will be put to death.

Antigone, the sister of Polyneices, rejects this decree outright. She performs burial rites for her brother so that he may find peace in the underworld. When she is caught, Creon orders her to be buried alive and rejects all appeals, including one by his own son Haemon, who is betrothed to Antigone.

Though Creon finally relents, it is too late. Antigone has killed herself, Haemon falls upon his own sword, and on receiving news of Haemon's death, Creon's wife also commits suicide. Creon is left in utter desolation.

Sophocles said all of this much more eloquently but these are the bare facts of the play's action. For me, the real power of this play comes in trying to answer two questions that surface regularly in different forms in my own life and work as a senator.

First, why did Creon fail to enrich his deliberations and thereby, perhaps, avoid tragedy and suffering?

Second, how might Creon—and Thebes itself—have avoided this failure and all the events that flowed from it?

We could substitute many names, including our own, for that of Creon. In fact, we must do so if we are to fulfill the goal of the author in creating understanding, in finding meaning, and gaining wisdom. We can and must do so because these questions go to the heart of human nature and to the foundation of our arrangements for governing ourselves.

There is no question that Creon's decree against the burial of Polyneices is unjust. It goes against established custom. It goes against the demands of the gods. It insults Antigone's duty to family and is an affront both to the citizenry of Thebes and the gods themselves.

Creon not only is willfully blind to his injustice, he compounds it by insisting that Antigone be put to death. He relents only when confronted by one who speaks with the authority of the gods. We are left to ask: Why did he not see, until too late, what was plain to everyone else?

There are several possible explanations for this behavior. But two are particularly compelling to me. One is Creon's confusion about the source and the limits of power. The other is his confusion about his own role as both giver and beneficiary of the law.

First, the issue of power. Creon's reason for the decree is based on Polyneices' actions against the state—his treasonous rebellion. If the state and the safety of its citizens are to be preserved, traitors must be punished. Surely, this reasoning is correct and Thebes owed no honor to one who sought to destroy it.

Creon's tragic error is in carrying this reasoning one step too far. He seeks not only to deny Polyneices the honor of the state, but the love of family. Thebes will not honor Polyneices and neither can Antigone. With this step, Creon crosses the narrow boundary between legitimate protection of the state and the use of state power in violating the rights—and duty—of an individual.

How often have we returned to this question: When may the state protect itself at the expense of the individual? In a real sense this is the sole question of government and all that is good or bad flows from our answer.

In addition to misjudging the limits of power, Creon confuses its source and its goal. As ruler of Thebes, Creon is the personification of the state. Creon *is* the state. Any crime against the state is a crime against Creon. Any challenge to Creon is a challenge to the state.

In these interlocking equations, which are well known in our own century, is the devastating danger of tyranny. From them spring authoritarianism and totalitarianism. They are the trapdoor through which liberty disappears.

Creon is eager to leap through this trapdoor and to take all Thebes with him. He is driven by the arrogance that comes with triumph, the pride that comes with power and, perhaps most of all, the angry, blinding self-righteousness of one who feels wronged.

Polyneices betrayed the state. He betrayed Creon. Therefore, he must be punished not only in life but in death, not only now but forever. The wickedness, the injustice of his actions becomes the foundation for the wickedness and injustice of the one he opposed.

In ways great and small, this cycle plays itself out time and again. The great tyrannies of our time, fascism and Marxism, were founded on the injustices that preceded them and that they proposed to redress.

Creon's eagerness to see himself as a victim and thereby justify his own actions is deeply rooted in human nature. If we are wronged, or at least feel wronged, we can assign blame to others; we can demand recompense; we can take a rightful place beneath the banner of justice and march proudly forward—even if we must trample others along the way.

In reading *Antigone*, there is a tendency to identify with Antigone herself as the true victim of the play. Despite the cold, self-centeredness of her idealism, we are attracted to her courage and the purity of her sense of duty. But if we admire Antigone's stance, we also must acknowledge that we frequently act more like Creon.

In our time, victim mentality seems to run rampant. We do not trust to Antigone's higher, unwritten law. We want it all spelled out in federal statutes. We increasingly are a society that focuses on the most minute details of our daily life. We regulate everything from the color of oranges to the size of eggs. We sue at the drop of a hat—not only the one who drops the hat but the hat manufacturer and the one who owns the place where it lands.

At times, we seem obsessed with achieving a perfect and pure justice. Nothing is to be left to chance and nothing is the result of chance. I do not suggest that we should ignore injustice or fail to protect our citizenry, but we should be mindful that true justice can never be measured in millimeters. In trying to make it so, we run risks as real as those Creon faced.

As Alexander Solzhenitsyn once warned: "When the tissue of life is woven of legalistic relations, there is an atmosphere of moral mediocrity, paralyzing man's noblest impulses."

Let me turn now—more briefly—to the second question I raised: How might Creon—and Thebes itself—have avoided this tragic conflict? My response to this is even more specifically rooted in my perspective as a twentieth century American.

What is missing in the conflict between Creon and Antigone is an effective force of moderation that can balance the competing good of one against the good of all.

If, as we Americans frequently feel, there must be a villain in this conflict, let me suggest an unusual one—the chorus, which represents the citizens of Thebes.

I was struck repeatedly by the passivity of the chorus—which I realize was not expected to be, in plays of the period, a major voice—and by extension the citizens of the state, to all that transpired right before their eyes. Creon would speak, the chorus would nod and murmur agreement. Antigone would speak, the chorus would nod and murmur agreement. At no time is the chorus required to choose a side and seek a resolution to a conflict in which they, the citizenry, held the highest stakes. Such intervention is left to the gods.

This passivity endures to our own time in many ways. Democracy increasingly seems to be a spectator sport. We have become a modern chorus that sits before the television to receive a sixty-second sound bite from the campaign. Then we nod and murmur agreement.

Fortunately, our Founding Fathers required that we eventually must choose a side by casting our ballots—though many of us choose simply not to do so. This has been our strong shield against the tyranny of either a Creon or an Antigone, and it has served us well. But I think both Sophocles and our Founding Fathers would expect more of us than a few minutes in a polling place.

Are we obligated not merely to listen and decide but to speak and so shape the final decision? If we expect more from those who would lead us than the current campaign has offered, is there no obligation to demand more? Or should we all just shrug and play our part as a docile chorus that is happy to choose our next president on the basis of a tour through a flag factory or a ride in a tank?

Thomas Jefferson and his contemporaries placed great faith—and enormous power—in the hands of their fellow citizens and in us. They did so in the belief that we could and would be the moderating force to prevent the tragedies of a long and dark past.

Jefferson's confidence was set down in these words: "I know of no safe depository of the ultimate powers of the society but the people themselves: and if we think them not enlightened enough to exercise their control with a wholesome discretion, the remedy is not to take it from them but to inform their discretion."

Jefferson made explicit the implied lesson of Sophocles in defining the duties of the citizen. We must listen well and exercise "a wholesome discretion." We also must speak wisely and so inform the discretion of our fellow citizens.

The tragedy of Creon and Antigone is that each refused to join in genuine dialogue, truly listening to one another. They refused to join in the struggle to balance their differences and instead insisted on emphasizing them and so polarizing each other.

The dangers of speaking without hearing, and hearing without speaking, remain with us even today. Each generation, and each individual, must learn again the wisdom spoken by Haemon to his father:

> Do not have one mind, and one alone that only your opinion can be right. Whoever thinks that he alone is wise, his eloquence, his mind, above the rest, come the unfolding, shows his emptiness. A man, though wise, should never be ashamed of learning more, and must unbend his mind.

JAMES BOND STOCKDALE

ON

Epictetus' Enchiridion

I was thirty-eight years old in 1962 when I first encountered the classic text that influenced my life. The book was Epictetus' *Enchiridion*, and we got off to a very unpromising start together. I just couldn't bring myself to see that what that old coot Epictetus had to say bore any relationship to my life as a twentieth century technocrat.

The book had special meaning because it was a gift from a man sixteen years my senior, whom I idolized. It was given to me by Philip Rhinelander, my professor of philosophy at Stanford University Graduate School. He had been my mentor for almost a year when, during my last tutorial session, he removed the little worn and marked-up personal volume from a high shelf in his study and said: "Here is a book that a man in your profession should own. Keep it and read it from time to time."

I was a career naval officer, an experienced fighter pilot about to return to sea duty to command a carrier-based squadron flying the navy's latest supersonic jets. What did I have in common with a first century Stoic who went along page after page reciting epigrams like:

Men are disturbed not by things but by the view they take of them.

Do not be concerned with things that are beyond your power.

Demand not that events should happen as you wish, but wish them to happen as they do happen and you will go on well.

Midcareer graduate education is not uncommon in military life, though it is somewhat rare to have it in a field entirely separate from one's immediate concerns. For nearly twenty years I had been on the operational and technical side of things—an engineering degree from Annapolis, with shore duty as an engineering test pilot bracketed by flying tours in carrier-based squadrons. I was now to return to such an aeronautical life after this sabbatical devoted to the study of political science, economics, and international relations with as much of the humanities as I could pack in. I did this in hopes of eventually achieving a high command that needed this education for policymaking and diplomatic and strategic planning duties.

I and others have found that a midlife second education, particularly one heavily salted with introspective subjects like classical philosophy, can precipitate an unexpected postgraduate wrinkle. An aftershock can develop as one returns to life in the world of cutting-edge technology, expediency, and not infrequent bureaucratic infighting. Throughout the first six or eight months after returning to the operational scene, I underwent a kind of transitional decompression. I groped for a stable platform of philosophical reference from which I could confidently call my shots. It wasn't because I was in a new environment that I had to screw my head on a new way; it was just that I now saw contradictions where before I had seen only order. I had to hook my life to a big idea if I was to stay the course.

It was now 1963. Throughout 1961 and 1962 at Stanford, my mind had been awhirl with a whole new shopping list of big ideas. Rhinelander's two-term philosophy course in "The Problems of Good and Evil" had alone taken me from the Book of Job to Camus, with more than a smattering of Plato, Aristotle, Shakespeare, Kant, Pascal, Leibnitz, Spinoza, Descartes, and Hume along the way. But now, as I led my squadron on and off the carrier decks in Southeast Asian waters, halfway between war and peace, I gravitated toward a more self-supporting, independent ethical balance wheel as I suffocated in the moral dilemmas that I could feel closing in on us all. There, my last-found model, Epictetus and his Stoicism, who by then I had made myself better understand, struck the very chord of self-respect and personal autonomy that I so needed to keep my mind clear and to break through the clutter of false hope and wishful thinking and to cut myself free.

Had I been an ancient Stoic, I would have expressed what roughly went through my mind like this: "Just as in the universe, where the mind of God is imminent and indwelling and moves in a manner self-sufficient and self-ruling, so I as the leader of pilots in times of unexpected change, frequent confusion, and occasional duplicity in high places, can do no better than to interpose myself between those pilots and our bumbling bureaucracy as their ultimate guide and protector. I must cast off concern for all things not within my power. Remembering that as I aim for such goals, I must not undertake them by acting moderately, but must let go from within myself that enigmatic mixture of conscience and egoism called honor, and not hesitate to make exceptions to operational rules and procedures as necessary to follow my eternal guides of duty and personal responsibility."

With such an outlook, 1963 and 1964, eerie years of national decision, were *not* times of great soul searching for me. I experienced one big soul search, embraced Stoicism, and was off and running; once I had made up my mind not to be concerned with things beyond my power, I was no longer hung up on where I began and where I left off in these enigmatic conditions. The conditions were tailor-made for Stoicism, and in my new-found freedom, tailor-made for me. I loved the life I lived during those years; it was unique in modern military history. Washington was determined to call every shot and their operations were compounding and stumbling over one another; normal business was crowded out and chaos frequently reigned. When caught in the crossfire of the conflicting imperatives of our secret missions into places like Laos, my conscience counseled: "Follow your duty as you interpret it, don't foolishly endanger your pilots, do what you think is best, improvise with confidence, and be prepared to stand accountable for your actions."

So it was on that most chaotic night of those years, August 4th, 1964, when Washington decided officially to go to war. Just before midnight, I had been the eyewitness with the best seat in the house to see an action that had been reported as an attack by North Vietnamese PT boats against the American destroyers, *Maddox* and *Joy*. It was, in fact, a false alarm caused by the destroyers' phantom radar contacts and faulty sonar operation on a very dark, humid, and stormy night. This was realized during the event by the boss of the destroyers at the scene, and by me, the boss of the airplanes overhead. Corrective messages were sent instantly to Washington: "No PT boats."

A few hours later, I was awakened to organize, brief, and lead the first air strike against North Vietnam, a reprisal for what I knew to be a false alarm. It was true that I had helped repulse an actual attack three days before, and that I thought it likely that another real one would occur in the future. But what to do, knowing that hours before, Washington had received the false-alarm messages, and that it would be none other than I who would be launching a war under false pretenses?

I remember sitting on the side of my shipboard bed, alone in those predawn minutes, conscious of the fact that history was taking a major turn, and that it was I, little Jimmy Stockdale, who happened to be in the ferris wheel seat that was just coming over the top and starting its descent. I remember two thoughts. The first was a pledge: that this was a moment to tell my grandchildren about some day, a history lesson important to future generations. The second was a reflection: I thought about Rhinelander, his "The Problems of Good and Evil" course, Epictetus and how prophetic it had been that we had all come together those few years before. Probably nobody had ever tested Rhinelander's course as I was likely to test it in not only the hours, but the years ahead. I knew we were stepping into a quagmire. There was no question of getting the truth of that night out; that truth had been out for hours. I was sure that there was nothing I could do to stop the "reprisal" juggernaut pouring out of Washington. My course was clear: to play well the given part. The Author had cast me in a lead role of a Greek tragedy. Who else to lead my pilots into the heavy flak of the city of Vihn and blow the North Vietnamese oil storage tanks off the map?

> Remember that you are an actor in a drama of such sort as the Author chooses—if short, then in a short one; if long, then in a long one. If it be his pleasure that you should enact a poor man, or a cripple, or a ruler, or a private citizen, see that you act it well. For this is your business—to act well the given part, but to choose it belongs to another.

So much for Stoicism as a guide to where one begins and where one leaves off in the world of free will. I now take leave of that relatively happy place, stale and jaded though it may have become in those years, and shift to the much worse circumstances of a political prison, a house of compulsion. There I found Stoicism an even more perfect fit.

I'm about to tell you more about the psychological side of life in a political prison than many of you will want to know. I assure you it isn't done for political instruction or shock effect but to take you inside the human mind in a state of its ultimate duress and show how Stoicism can elevate the dignity of man even in worst-case scenarios.

I got to that political prison just a little over a year after I blew those tanks off the map. (The Tonkin Gulf Resolution had been passed by the Congress two days later, and the air war in North Vietnam was on.) It was on September 9, 1965, after a couple of hundred bombing missions in that war (and just three years after I left graduate school), that my airplane was finally shot out of the sky. I arrived at the old French dungeon called Hoa Lo ("Fiery Furnace") Prison in Hanoi, as a stretcher case, three days later.

I identify Hoa Lo as a political prison rather than a "P.O.W. camp," not just because of its honeycomb of tiny cells, each with a cement-slab bed, leg irons at its foot, a food chute above the irons, a toilet bucket beside, and a "rat hole" to the outside drainage ditch for flushing, but because it was a place where people are sent to be used, to have their minds changed, or both. Political prisons are not to be confused with penitentiaries or prison camps where people are locked up to preserve the public peace or pay their debts to society. Little attention is given to terms of confinement or time schedules. They are institutions devoted only to the discrediting of the inmates' causes; when all the prisoner's juices have been squeezed out, when his forced confession of crimes never committed are judged as convincing as they can be made to be, he is usually free to go. (It's not generally known, but Americans held in Hanoi were free to go any time, provided that the prisoner (1) cut juicy enough anti-American tapes, *and* (2) he was then willing to violate our prisoners' underground organization's self-imposed creed of comradeship: "Accept no parole or amnesty; we all go home together." Thus we came to imprison ourselves, for honor, in accordance with our Code of Conduct. I might add that this mystified several high officials of our government here in Washington. They didn't know their own Code.)

Given their charge, the breaking of human will, all political prisons are similar. That is to say, neither what goes on there, nor how their prey grapple with it, appreciably change, century in and century out: Cervantes', Dostoevsky's, and my accounts are all the same. At the heart of the organization is a master extortionist or commissar like Gletkin of *Darkness at Noon* and the Cat of *In Love and War*. The same methods are used now as were used in the Middle Ages. They don't use drugs; they want to impose guilt; they want authenticity with no easy outs or plausible denials. They do not use brainwashing; there is no such thing. They do use pain, administered by a few selected torture guards. They also use isolation. Such prisons use a trip-wire system of multitudinous regulations, some of which many inmates inadvertently break because of their number and ambiguity, and other regulations which almost all inmates eventually intentionally break because their requirements defy human nature. (In particular, there was a regulation for us never to communicate in any way with another American prisoner.) The idea in political prisons is to *get* prisoners to break regulations. Since any violation is considered, prima facie, moral turpitude or "evidence of ingratitude," it is used as justification to recycle the inmate through the torture meat grinder. From that, the commissars obtain, on a production line basis, confessions, apologies, and atonements.

Seasoned veterans of these regimes realize that pain and isolation, to say nothing of other deprivations and miseries, are mere accelerators to the major pincers of this will-breaking machine: imposed fear and guilt. "Destabilize with fear, polarize with guilt," say the graffiti on the cave walls of the alchemists of the Middle Ages who worked on psychic transformation under pressure. In fact, the total regime comes to seem to its sufferers like an alchemist's hermetically sealed, pressurized, and heated retort, in which they are perpetually stalked, hounded down, and harpooned with barbs of fear and guilt.

Like all good squeeze-play systems, political prisons are meant to destroy the man who chooses the "middle way," who decides to be "reasonable," to "meet them half-way." For hours on end, my commissar would plead with me to follow that track: "You are an American, you are pragmatic; come, let us reason together." It is only when he can get you to level with him in some small way, to drop your guard and betray an emotional dependence on his good will, that he can get his crowbars of fear and guilt behind your armor and begin to twist.

Political prison extortion is one grand leverage game. The inmate is well served to chant the rules he must live by under his breath: "Show no fear." "Never trigger shame." "The credibility of your defiance must be maintained." "The prison onslaught must be contained." "Never level with a jailer." One soon learns that to survive with self-respect, he has to divest himself of the remnants of his student-body-president personality: the willingness to be open, to interact, to respond in interesting ways. With time and care, many prisoners create a new independent personality that even under torture is difficult to manipulate. In Stoic terms, having external needs makes one vulnerable and vulgar.

> The condition and characteristic of a vulgar person is that he never looks for either help or harm from himself, but only from externals. The condition and characteristic of a [Stoic] philosopher is that he looks to himself for all help or harm.

I do not suggest that I understood all this while in prison or that the *Enchiridion* was familiar enough to use as a text on how to face the challenge. But, remembering my experiences in prison, I have since come to think that the *Enchiridion* has all the right answers.

On the tactical side, the main idea I bring away from Epictetus is to "stay off the hook." If a prisoner demands conveniences, accepts favors, pleads for relief, aspires to status, attempts to prove something about himself to others, this means giving a manipulator an opening through showing need for "externals." The smart inmate makes it his business to find his tormentor's exact limits, to know his own, and to demonstrate a commitment his adversary finds it unprofitable to challenge.

> A man's master is he who is able to confer or remove whatever that man seeks or shuns. Whoever then would be free, let him wish nothing, let him decline nothing which depends on others; else he must necessarily be a slave.

Shun externals, yes. But a man must concern himself in the world of Epictetus and in the world of extortion and manipulation with "internals," or those matters that are "up to him," and only to him.

> Our opinions are up to us, our impulses, desires, aversions—in short whatever is of our own doing.

Viktor Frankl, in *Man's Search for Meaning*, speaks of the "freedom" he found, even in the depths of terror in his Nazi prison, in realizing that there was one thing they could never take from him: his attitude and his opinion of what was going on. As Jean-Paul Sartre said to a priest in another Nazi prison, "Remember, the important thing in here is not what they do to you, but what *you* do with what they do to you."

Internals are man's only true ticket to freedom, but confronting them can be agonizing. In prison, there is one internal decision that is difficult beyond all others: when to first say "no" and knowingly force the commissar's hand to carry out his threats and impose physical torture. This turning point almost always takes place in a frenzied moment when the new prisoner is awash in a sea of guilt and fear. The guilt arises from his having "gone along" with the commissar's demand for a little of this and a little of that, while in the fashion of most of us well-brought-up American boys he had chosen "the middle way," to his now devastating regret, as he took preliminary measure of his predicament. And the fear! Arthur Koestler, while in a Fascist prison in Spain, described his initial fear of torture as "not a healthy fear, but the obsessional and morbid variety . . . the neurotic type of anxiety . . . the irrational anticipation of an unknown punishment."

No men avoid this initial terrible fear that only their imaginations can generate and few, if any, avoid the initial hesitant step of grudgingly giving ground while taking measure of their predicament. Finding himself sinking into the quagmire of complicity, hardly a man exists who does not wish he had stood up and blown the "enough's enough" whistle sooner than he did. For self-respect—and in the long-term sense, for mental health—the sooner he blows the whistle, the better.

> If a person had delivered up your body to some passer by, you would certainly be angry. And do you feel no shame in delivering up your mind to any reviler, to be disconcerted and confounded?
>
> It is better to die of hunger, exempt from guilt and fear, than to live in affluence with perturbation.
>
> If a man's sense of honour, his good faith, and his prudence are not destroyed, then he too is preserved; but if *any* of these perish or be taken by storm, then he too perishes with them.

Once the neophyte political prisoner realizes that experiencing pain is not as bad as its anticipation, a kind of equanimity and pride comes over him. He knows that it is the unpunished complicity, not the tortured compliance, that tears a man apart. He casts aside the error of involving himself with externals, of depending on, "what is not up to him," on another's sympathy, gullibility, or price for making a "deal." He uses both the rational and irrational elements of his soul—both part of the same to the Stoic—to see his proper role in the unfolding drama. He accommodates himself to fate. He makes a declaration to himself and to the prison regime that, regarding his choices, he is "free." He has arrived at the point where the "strategic" side of Stoicism, the accommodation to fate and mind over matter, can bring him peace.

To the Stoics, God and the visible universe are two aspects of the same thing. God's Soul is the Mind, and the visible universe, nature, is his body. The Mind is the divine reason, immanent in the universe, whose nature reveals itself in the imperturable laws of Nature. As humans, we are all a part not only of the visible universe, but our minds are a part of the Mind. The Mind, the universal, divine, all-embracing consciousness, is like a flame, and our individual consciousnesses are sparks in it. Hence each of us has a divine element in him. Just as God's Soul, or the Mind, is the active principle of the universe, and his body, or Nature, is passive, so are our minds the active principle in us, and our bodies passive. Mind over matter; it all happens up here, don't worry about your body. Also, there is no chance in the Stoic ordering of things. All that happens is inevitable, proceeding for God's nature. By using the divine elements in us, we can know how nature proceeds from God's Mind by divine necessity. A free man is one who understands this and accommodates himself to fate. The good man plays well the part fate has dealt him.

Stoicism is certainly not for everybody, and it is not for me in every circumstance, but it is an expression in philosophical terms of how people find purpose in what they have every right to see as a purposeless world. This is certainly the world of those who find themselves in that ever-proliferating human institution, the political prison. But Stoicism has apt application well beyond that population. It speaks to people everywhere who persist in competing in what they see as a buzz-saw existence, their backs to the wall, their lives having meaning only so long as they fight for pride with comradeship and joy rather than capitulate to either tyranny or phoniness.

In recent years I have been working on books that are heavily focused on my ten years in Vietnam. Publishers always ask writers to think through such questions as: "What in your background can you connect with this or that impulsive action?" or ". . . this or that decision?" I date most of the dramatic, intuitive material to the frustrations, fears, or guilts I incurred as a young boy. The intellectual decisions are harder to place, but the liberal arts ("as much of the humanities as I could pack in") at Stanford undoubtedly allowed me to be more comfortable writing my own rule book as I dealt with unusual circumstances, than had I stuck with high tech all the way. But it was Epictetus who played the unique part in preparing me for all this. I walked in his shoes throughout that time. Particularly in the prison scene, he was my guide for ethics, but more importantly, a guide to outlook, psychology, and will. One of the most valuable memories I had was that of recalling, even if faintly, that serious scholarship existed about a breed of men devoted to a Principle of Life of staying off the hook and prevailing with pride and joy against all odds in a hopeless world.

So it was that in Hanoi, after each of us in his solitude brought about his crucial rite of passage from the neurotic anxiety of the vestibule to the comforting pain of the star chamber, he joined a brotherhood of Stoics, dedicated to keeping high the spirits of each other, while locked in combat against hopeless odds, under the banner, "stick it in their ear." We flaunted the trip wire, made them torture us, and prevailed in establishing a civilization of men held together by a network of clandestine wall-tap communication. This civilization matured rapidly, as do all things in the pressurized hermetic, hot box, and took on all the usual binding elements of a culture: its own tap code dialect, traditions, heroes, inside jokes, and, of course, laws, leaders, and specific rules regarding succession to command.

My name appears to this day in official navy records as a man whose government-paid postgraduate education was never utilized. The bureaucracy scores my twenty-four months at Stanford a waste of money because I was shot down before I ever had a chance to take that Washington job they had in mind for me. How tunnel visioned can you get? What better preparation for head-of-government of an autonomous colony for nearly eight years than prior concentrated study on "The Problems of Good and Evil?" And the lessons of Epictetus paid off in pure gold.

The hardships were many, bones were broken, death visited some, but most of us were sure, deep inside, that we were on the right track by staying with internals, refusing to make deals, building a clandestine civilization, and seeking and finding purpose in serving each other in an otherwise purposeless world.

> Difficulties are what show men's character. Therefore, when a difficult crisis meets you, remember that you are as the raw youth whom God the trainer is wrestling.

To the person skeptical of the validity of this Stoic approach to life in this aspect of war, I add one assertion: no psychotics came out with us. Every man felt good about himself. That's the difference.

*　　　*　　　*

Did I undergo another transitional decompression, a reordering of values, as I reentered this modern world of freedom? The answer is no. I couldn't generate the same kind of turmoil in my mind that occurred when I first reentered the world of bureaucratic infighting and expediency from the halls of Stanford's philosophy corner. I was happy with the philosophic tilt I brought out of prison. I was by then wise enough to know that Epictetus has his applications out here in what, after years of solitary confinement in total silence, I immediately dubbed the big wide noisy world of yackety-yack.

Once you've spent a few years as a target for the harpoons of fear and guilt in the hermetic hotbox of a political prison, you develop a very keen sensitivity for the first hints of the onset of an extortionistic squeeze play. We who are in hierarchies—be they academic, business, military, or otherwise—are always in positions in which people are trying to manipulate us, to get moral leverage on us. The only defense is to keep yourself clean—never to do or say anything of which you can be made to feel ashamed. A smart and ethical person never gives a manipulator an even break. He is always prepared to quench the extortionist's artful insinuation of guilt with the ice water of a truthful, clear-conscienced put-down. The more benign the environment, the more insidious is the extortionist's style. How true the Arthurian legend: "Then Arthur learned, as all leaders are astonished to learn, that peace, not war, is the destroyer of men; that tranquility, rather than danger, is the mother of cowardice; and that not need, but plenty, brings apprehension and unease."

Epictetus' tactics, particularly that of staying off the hook, are very good advice for those who seek dignity in our modern bureaucratized society. A few years ago, I originated and taught a course at Stanford entitled "Combatting Coercion and Manipulation." Though we concentrated on applications of the course in everyday life, I chose our case studies not from office politics but from prison literature, such as the trial and death of Socrates, the confrontation of Christ by Dostoevsky's Grand Inquisitor, the interrogations of Koestler's Commissar Rubashov by Ivanov and Gletkin, *A Day in the Life of Ivan Denisovich*, and Epictetus' and my own saga. Stoicism was a matter of deep curiosity to the students. There was much discussion about the sense of freedom and dignity it can spawn, about how its adherents so differed from moderns in never thinking of themselves as victims, and about its being a seedbed for the idea of the brotherhood of men, who share common status as humans, who are born with innate and highly principled ideas and with a touch of the divine.

> For we come into this world with no innate conception of a right-angled triangle, or of a quarter-tone or of a semi-tone, but we are taught what each of these means by systematic instruction; and therefore those who are ignorant of these things do not think that they know them. On the other hand every one has come into the world with an innate conception as to good and bad, noble and shameful, becoming and unbecoming, happiness and unhappiness, fitting and inappropriate, what is right to do and what is wrong.

Am I personally still hooked on Epictetus' Principle of Life? Yes, but not in the sense of following a memorized doctrine. I sometimes become amused at how I have applied it and continue to apply it unconsciously. An example is the following story about myself.

As the months and years wear on in solitary confinement, it turns out that a man goes crazy if he doesn't get some ritual into his life. I mean by that a self-imposed obligation to do certain things in a certain order each day. Like most prisoners, I prayed some each day, month after month, continually altering and refining a long memorized monologue that probably ran to ten or fifteen minutes. At some point, my frame of mind became so pure that I started deleting any begging of God and any requests of God that would work specifically for my benefit. This didn't come out of any new Principle of Life that I had developed; it just suddenly started to seem unbecoming to beg. I knew the lesson of the Book of Job: life is not fair. What claim had I for special consideration? And anyway, by then I had seen enough misery to realize that He had enough to worry about without trying to appease a crybaby like me. And so it has been ever since.

I never thought about the implications of this until recently when I reread *A Day in the Life of Ivan Denisovich*, and it struck home that the simple soldier Ivan thinks it immoral to ask God for more than daily bread. It suddenly dawned on me: How Stoic can you get? Ivan and I, so different in culture, he never alone, I always alone, yet each drawing on a wisdom born of extortion and hardship, a wisdom best articulated two thousand years ago by our common ancestor in hardship, a crippled Greek slave. Through Epictetus, Ivan and I became brothers.

Messages like these come only through the classics.

Of the teachers in this audience, I ask: Isn't this the ultimate appeal of the classics? Their lessons are applicable to all ages, and this is true because they dwell on unchanging human nature. As you know, some in intellectual circles like to think there is no such thing as human nature, others fancy it can be changed, and some even believe they themselves can bring about the change! I met some highly placed educators at a recent curriculum-planning conference on how to educate leaders for the twenty-first century who said: "Wow, in the twenty-first century, all previous bets are off!" "It's a completely new ball game." "The world of individuality and ego has got to go; we've got to erase these outmoded bad habits of several thousand years and get everybody pacified and cooperative." "Put away that curriculum you brought, Stockdale, that reading list with all those old books." "No more old books!"

Of course, these educators are social scientists, who write prolifically about something called "values." They don't read Aristotle's *Politics* because they believe that what comes out of Harvard's Kennedy Center is more relevant. They don't read Aristotle's *Ethics* because they believe that books about cognitive development are better. Some teachers believe that in concentrating on contemporary trendy material they are announcing new ideas, scientifically demonstrated by something called "research," and that they are thereby helping to save the world. Actually they are spreading indifference and lassitude in their classrooms because they are talking about a contrived race of people that do not live. Remember the poet W. H. Auden's parting commandment to us in the United States as he left these shores for his native England, "Thou shalt not commit a social science!"

As I have already indicated, my reading list for a person about to enter circumstances entailing high risk of political imprisonment would be Cervantes, Dostoevsky, and Koestler, rather than the latest "how to" government handout. But to prepare best for the life I have lived, I should have been reading Homer, not Mahan, at the Naval Academy. Hector is about to leave the gates of Troy to fight Achilles. He will lose, and he will die. When he says goodbye to his wife and baby son by the gate, the baby starts to cry as he becomes frightened by the "nodding" of the plumes on his father's shining helmet bobbing in the breeze. You have it all in that instantaneous snapshot: Hector's duty, his wife's tragedy, Troy's necessity, the baby's cry. In the *Iliad* we can discern our family's life in the twentieth century—the life we really live. The material of the classics has human meaning because it centers on a human nature that mutates, if at all, only with glacier-like leisureliness.

You ask what can a teacher do, using a text like the *Enchiridion*, to open a student's mind and heart to respond to the claim the text wants to make on his or her life? Suppose brotherhood is the subject.

Enchiridion:

Everything has two handles: one by which it can be borne, another by which it cannot. If your brother does you wrong, don't lay hold on the situation by the handle of his doing you wrong, for by that you cannot bear it, but rather by the opposite—that he is your brother.

Does that not give a clearer, more human answer to the age-old question of Cain to the Almighty: "Am I my brother's keeper?" than the following from a current book on "teaching values"?

The stage six reasoner views an individual's rights in much the same manner as would a stage five reasoner but with a much greater emphasis on the respect for life and personality of the individual.

Of course, that's not a fair comparison, some would say. We need to know what stage five is, what stage six is, and also stages one, two, and three, and more if we are to have (as this textbook from which I'm unfairly quoting would have us have) a proper appreciation for the cognitive developmental approach to moral teaching.

When I was lying for months with a broken back and a broken leg, sick, without medical treatment, in solitary confinement, I vividly remember getting a real boost from remembering a few simple lines from the *Enchiridion*:

> Sickness is an impediment to the body, but not to the will. Lameness is an impediment to the leg, but not to the will.

You teachers can fill in the blanks with the names of all those men and women you know who have transcended the crippling effects of disease or injury and gone on to do things that the world would be so much the poorer without.

This last word is to teachers and nonteachers alike. Tell your kids this and see that they don't forget it. It is from chapter 35 of the *Enchiridion*:

> When you do anything from a clear judgment that it ought to be done, never shrink from being seen to do it, even though the world should misunderstand it; for if you are not acting rightly, shun the action itself; but if you are, why fear those who wrongly censure you?

WILLIAM J. RICHARDSON, S.J.

ON

Teaching Epictetus

My task is to respond to Admiral Stockdale and in doing so to propose one way of making the text of Epictetus meaningful to students. It would seem to me that it would be a fairly easy task to engage students in a basic interest in the text simply because of Admiral Stockdale himself. I would try to share with them my own experience, which I am sure that you share, too, of a certain feeling of awe, certainly of humility, of deference in the presence of someone like Admiral Stockdale, who so clearly is the archetypical American hero, a winner of the Congressional Medal of Honor who has survived long enough to tell us why he deserved it so richly. I would make much, then, of Admiral Stockdale as a person and in terms of the phrase that was used yesterday afternoon about the text speaking through a lived transparency. It would seem that Admiral Stockdale himself is both the text and the transparency that has lived before us. And it is the presence, therefore, of a very great man that I would attempt to help the students to experience, to understand what it is to be in the presence of the real thing.

That said, I would, of course, try first to explain something about Epictetus himself. Admiral Stockdale has already given us a pen picture, so to speak, of Epictetus, and he has told us about as much as we know of him as a person. I would then get quickly into the text itself, having indicated, just to situate him at the beginning of the early empire, that Epictetus was one of the later Stoics, taking his place along with Seneca and Marcus Arelius. The chronology would give an opportunity to say that the texts of Plato and Aristotle, with all their power, had by 300 BC lost their hold on the intellectual culture of Greece. They had gone into a kind of decline to be replaced by philosophies that could not match their level of intellectual speculation and that settled for a way to come to grips with the trials and tribulations of life.

I would then try to suggest that simply looking for a way to live in the world supposes that some kind of theoretical foundation be taken seriously. I would therefore try to point out the broader dimensions of the theory of stoicism that Admiral Stockdale has summarized so concisely and so clearly. I would try to say that actually the Stoics were struggling for some kind of philosophical, not to say metaphysical, basis, but the best they could do was to rehash something that had already had its day and was ready to be revived, namely the thought of Heraclitus. The Stoics conceived that what Heraclitus talked about as the primordial ingredient of the cosmos was essentially a fire. Now it is not at all clear that Heraclitus himself really meant a physical fire, but the Stoics seem to have taken it quite literally, and therefore, for the Stoics, the world emerged out of a primordial fire into the cosmos that we experience to return again into a primordial fire out of which, at another epic of time, the cycle would begin again in a kind of eternal return.

I would insist, therefore, that in this space that we occupy between fire and fire, there is a certain order and cosmos controlled by what Heraclitus called the logos, what others would call simply spirit. In any case, some principle of order made this cosmos as we experience it a highly harmonic, totally organized, totally coherent universe. I would insist that, after all, the stoics were talking about some kind of monistic explanation of the cosmos and, therefore, of life. I would point out that for them man was really a part of this material process, and if he had an intellect and a will that distinguished him from animals, these were sort of scintillae of the original fire which had their place in him and by reason of which he could do the best he could both to live in this harmonious order and to accommodate to this harmonious order (of which he was a part) by accepting what he could not control and by controlling as much as he could and making his peace with it. I would therefore cite the texts that Admiral Stockdale cites at the beginning of his talk, "Men are disturbed not by things, but by the view that they take of them. Do not be concerned with things that are beyond your power. Demand not that events should happen as you wish, but wish them to happen as they do happen and you will go on well." The sense, therefore, would be to try to indicate that what peace comes to a Stoic comes out of an accommodation to necessity which he cannot escape and with which he must make his peace.

Then I would underline a little bit the theme that Admiral Stockdale makes a great deal of: the difference between the externals and the internals and staying off the hook. I would hope that the students would see the power of his statement: "What you need is a personality that does not betray a dependence on externals, on others. To have external psychic needs is to be vulnerable, in Stoic terms, to be vulgar." And then he cites Epictetus, "The condition and characteristics of a vulgar person is that he never looks for either help or harm from himself, but only from externals. The condition and characteristics of a [Stoic] philosopher is that he looks to himself for all help or harm." And I would try to draw that statement out and explore its implications: "He looks to himself for all help." Admiral Stockdale said, "There comes a time when you have to say, 'No' to the seductions of the interrogator, when you have to blow the whistle." But there are different ways of blowing the whistle, and there is one issue in Epictetus that doesn't come up in Admiral Stockdale's paper. I would call that issue to the attention of the students and let them see and feel its appeal: "To sum up," says Epictetus, "remember that the door is open. Do not be a greater coward than the children, but do as they do. Children, when things do not please them, say, 'I will not play anymore.' So when things seem to you to reach that point, just say, 'I'll not play anymore,' and so depart," and don't go on moaning. Well, that poses, therefore, obviously, the question of suicide, and so in the presence of my students, I would raise the question, "Why not commit suicide? What's wrong with suicide? Why do you think Admiral Stockdale did not commit suicide? Would it have been a viable option?" I would, therefore, force the issue of what freedom really means in a situation like that. How many options do you really have?

In any case, Admiral Stockdale points out the effect of an Epictetian approach to the presence of pain that comes from torture, and he speaks in very poignant terms of the equanimity and pride, of a sense of dignity and, above all, a sense of freedom that comes in a situation like that. He says at one point, "Accommodation to fate" and "mind over matter" can bring peace. At another point he says, "Internals [that is to say, living for the internals] are man's only true ticket to freedom." What price freedom? "What does it really mean to be free?" I would ask. And in exploring the notion of freedom, I would try to pose the problem as crucially as possible. What does it really mean to be free? Does it really mean more than what the Stoics offer us: namely, the acceptance of an ineluctable necessity. Is our only freedom to say yes to this necessity? Is that sufficient? Is that what you mean by free will? And when Admiral Stockdale uses the phrase free will today, does he mean something more than that?

I would also take the opportunity to say that this position is not unique to Epictetus. It is characteristic of many a philosopher who has come, let us say, to find freedom only in acceptance of an ineluctable necessity. I would point to Spinoza. I would point to Hegel. I would point to Marx and make reference to Sakharov. I would point to Freud. What kind of freedom does psychoanalysis offer it if is not acceptance of the ineluctable necessity of the unconscious having its way with you? You can make a case for its being the freedom that Heidegger offers. What, then, really is freedom? And what kind of price are you willing to pay for it? That historical perspective might be implemented if circumstances permitted, and it would be a judgment call, mind you, but it would be interesting to have students see the import of the notion of this logos operating in the life of a person, because this logos, after all, is law. It is the law. It is also nature. It is the law of nature, and therefore the natural law is simply accommodating to this law of nature as it is experienced here.

Students could see, then, I would think, the role of stoicism in the thought of St. Thomas and I would encourage them to see as well as its role in any attempt to talk about natural law subsequent to St. Thomas. I might also point to the role and the seduction of stoicism in the whole history of Christian spirituality, particularly during the later Renaissance, when Renaissance thinkers returned to models of Greek and Roman perfection as criteria of their own perfection. And I think it would be an interesting thing, especially if some of the students were clearly Catholic, still more if they were seminarians, to point out that a careful study ought to be made among the ascetical writers of the 16th, 17th and 18th century and particularly (although I'm not sure Father Gray would agree with me) among the interpreters of *The Spiritual Exercises* of St. Ignatius about the role of stoicism in Christian spirituality. We are posing, therefore, the question, "What does it really mean to be a Christian ascetic?"

I would then pass quickly to some kind of evaluation of Epictetus in the light of what Admiral Stockdale has offered us. His testimony was so eloquent that all you really can do, as Ken Eble put it, is to get out of the way and let students work with its implications by themselves. But two questions occur to me. The first is fairly easy to ask, and the second is a lot harder. The first question would be that when Admiral Stockdale says, at a given point, as a form of ritual to keep his sanity in solitary confinement, he began to pray, I would wonder what kind of a god he prays to as a Stoic. I find this awkward to ask, because it seems to me too personal, and I'm not asking Admiral Stockdale for an answer. I am posing the question to my students. Is it this kind of a god: "O God, most glorious, called by many a name, nature's great king through endless years the same, omnipotence who, by thy just decree, controllest all. Hail, Zeus."? Because Zeus was one of the names that the Stoics gave to the logos, to nature, and, therefore, I would wonder whether or not the prayer that Admiral Stockdale speaks of is a prayer to a personal god. And I would wonder, therefore, whether you really need a god who is personal in order to survive an experience like that. What does prayer mean? And when, with the tapping, he says, "Hi, God bless you," what kind of a god is that, because a Stoic god does not bless. And, therefore, I am wondering what is the role of a personal god *vis-à-vis* the Stoic experience. And is the appeal to a personal god or a god at all, even an imaginary god, that is to say, the logos given the name of God, is that anything more than what Freud tells us is a purely human need: one heeds some kind of father and, therefore, constructs an image to which he pays a certain obeisance only because he has not yet accepted fully the rigor of an absolutely stoic solution?

The second question, I say, is much harder to pose, because I would go back to a text which I found a little disconcerting. Let me read it to you, and I will explain why the question is harder to pose.

> So it was on that most chaotic night of all nights of those years, August 4th, 1964, when Washington decided officially to go to war. Just before midnight, I had been the eyewitness with the best seat in the house to see an action which had been reported as an attack by the North Vietnamese PT boats against the American destroyers *Maddox* and *Joy*. It was, in fact, a false alarm brought about by the destroyer's phantom radar contacts and faulty sonar operation and a very dark, humid and stormy night. This was realized during the event by the boss of the destroyers at the scene and by me, the boss of the airplanes overhead. Corrective messages were sent instantly to Washington: "No PT boats."
>
> A few hours later, I was awakened to organize, brief and lead the first air strike against North Vietnam, a reprisal for what I knew to be the false alarm. It was true that I had helped repulse an actual attack three days before, and that I thought it likely that another real one would occur in the future. But what to do, knowing that hours before, Washington had received the false alarm messages, and that it would be none other than I who would be launching a war under false pretenses.
>
> I remember sitting on the side of my shipboard bed, all alone in those pre-dawn minutes, fully conscious of the fact that history was taking a major turn, and it was I, little Jimmy Stockdale, who happened to be in the ferris wheel seat that was just coming over the top and starting its descent. I remember two thoughts of those

minutes. The first was a pledge: that this was an instant that I was going to tell my grandchildren about someday. I was living through a history lesson that would be important to future generations. The second was a reflection: I thought about Rhinelander and *"The Problems of Good and Evil"* and Epictetus and how prophetic it had been that we had all come together those very few years before. Probably nobody had ever tested Rhinelander's course as I was likely to test it, in not only the hours ahead, but the years ahead. I knew we were stepping into a quagmire. There was no question of getting the truth of that night out; that truth had been out for hours. I was sure that there was nothing I could do to stop the "reprisal" juggernaut pouring out of Washington. My course was clear: to play well the given part. The Author had cast me in a lead role of a Greek tragedy. Who else to lead my pilots into the heavy flack of the city of Vihn and blow the North Vietnamese oil storage tanks off the map?

Then, quoting Epictetus, Admiral Stockdale continues, "Remember that you are an actor in a drama of such sort that the Author chooses. If short, then in a short one; if long, then in a long one. If it be his pleasure that you should enact a poor man, or a cripple, or a ruler, or a private citizen, see that you act it well. For this is your business: to act well the given part, but to choose it belongs to another." Now I would post that statement in all starkness to the students and say, "How about that? How about that?" Is this a question of following orders? We have seen a history about people saying, *"Befehl ist Befehl,* orders are orders." And so I'd wonder, does it change things when the Author is capitalized and it happens to be the logos of a Stoic, Zeus. And I'd be very sensitive to, I'm very sensitive now, I hope you can see that I'm finding it very difficult to formulate this. I'm very sensitive to the anguish that question poses when those order come through. I would simply want the students to appreciate that anguish and ask them what would they do. And if they're really hell bent on stoicism, I would ask them, "What are your criteria of what's to do and what's not to do?" But my task would be simply to pose the question starkly to the students and not pretend to have an easy answer at all.

RENÉE POUSSAINT

ON

Machiavelli's "The Prince"

I'm very happy to be here this afternoon. I'm happy and somewhat surprised to have been invited since the general view of most people in television is that we are brain dead. There may be some merit to that, actually. The question is whether we're born that way, or whether we get that way because of the lights.

This day illustrates what most of my days in my business are like, and why I love my job. I will be talking about Machiavelli here. I will leave here and go down to Police District Headquarters to do a special on drug abuse in our community and the problems of drugs that are killing our children, and I will leave there and go back to the studio and do a news broadcast which will present certain segments of reality, and probably a somewhat distorted picture. Part of that picture will involve the presidential elections and what candidates are doing.

I had to go back to the typewriter and make some changes in the draft of this talk after watching last weekend's presidential debates. After all, the skeptical journalist in me said, "What could be more apropos of a televised political heavy weight bought in the 20th century than the words of 16th century diplomat and political analyst Niccolo di Bernardo Machiavelli?" He would certainly tend to be more blunt in his commentary than most modern day TV analysts.

While watching the debate, a particular segment from *The Prince* came to mind, probably because for the past few months as I've traveled the country covering primaries and the Democratic and Republican conventions, I've had to focus so much on the process of mutual manipulation between the candidates, the equivalent of our modern princes, and the media. I've had even more than my usual opportunity to see the differences between the man and the televised image of the man, and I've had plenty of troubling moments as I saw how difficult it was for the public, or as Machiavelli would say, the people to distinguish between those two images and sort out what is, in fact, real.

The passage from *The Prince* comes as Machiavelli discusses the five qualities people would like to have: ". . . mercy, faithfulness, integrity, kindness, and religious commitment." Machiavelli then goes on to say, however, ". . . it is not necessary for a prince to have all of the above-mentioned qualities, but it is very necessary to appear to have them. A Prince must be very careful," he says, "never to let anything slip from his lips which is not full of the five qualities mentioned above." He continues, "Everyone sees what you seem to be; few perceive what you are."

Telling words for a person like me whose livelihood is based on a medium that deals in creating illusions, a medium where the lines between news and entertainment become more blurred every day, where fact and fiction blend into a catchy new version of reality in something called "docu-dramas." Yes. Machiavelli has considerable relevance for me.

He may not, however, have been one of the authors the organizers of this symposium had in mind when they graciously invited me to participate. They simply said the talk should center around the personal encounter of an individual and a classic text. No particular text was specified. That was left up to me which, of course, given my nature and my Sarah Lawrence liberal arts education, immediately made me ask questions about how you define a classic—the same kind of questions that have been raised in recent months at any number of college campuses, including my own alma mater.

You've all, I'm sure, heard and read about the furor over the classics that hit Stanford University last spring, a furor centering around the university's Freshman Western Culture courses with a roster of 15 prescribed classics ranging from Homer and Dante to Darwin and Freud. A number of concerned faculty and students at Stanford pointed out that all 15 works were by white, western males, a fairly Euro-centric and biased sampling of western culture. They pushed to have a broader, more theme based program cutting down on the standard works and increasing contributions by non-Europeans and by women. The battle got fierce, spreading well beyond just one campus, the so-called revisionists being denounced by none other than our former Secretary of Education, William Bennett. And Steven Block, President of the National Association of Scholars called the whole trend ". . . intellectual affirmative action." (One of my favorite phrases.)

But at Stanford, at least, the revisionists won. The faculty senate voted 39 to 40 in favor of their compromise program, and I am in favor of the revisionists. For me, as a black woman, a classic text would include, for instance, works by James Baldwin, Alice Walker, Maya Anjalou, Du Bois, Chenuwa Chebe, Richard Wright, Tony Morrison—the list goes on. They are the voices of my culture. They are the ones who speak eternal truths. For those who would know what it is to be a black American in this time and in this place, how it is that we have evolved to where we now stand, they should experience some of those works.

How in the world, you might be wondering then, do I move from that context and that imperative to Machiavelli? The answer is not simple. In a way, for me to deal with one of the above-mentioned works would be almost too easy, too expected, too stereotypical. They would fit me like old, comfortable shoes. Machiavelli is not comfortable. We have a very troubling relationship, but one that has been of long duration and has had tremendous impact on my life.

To help you to understand, I must go back in time to explain to you a little of who I am and what I am, and how the work of a man seemingly so foreign to me could be so deeply a part of me. I was told not to give an academic lecture, which is a relief, because I am not qualified to do that. But instead, to give a very personal, anecdotal account of how a particular classic text consistently affected my life, my judgments, my vision of the world. The more I thought about it, the more I returned to Machiavelli, though not because I am a particularly Machiavellian personality. As a matter of fact, I am probably just the opposite. Rather, because Machiavelli has consistently forced me to come to terms with who I am, and what I really believe by confronting me with some harsh realities that grated on my consciousness, if not my very soul.

That may sound like a melodramatic overstatement, so let me put it into my context. I was raised a good little Catholic girl of working class parents in New York's Spanish Harlem. I spent my summers down South with my grandfather, a Baptist minister. Christianity, morality, absolutes in terms of right and wrong, good and evil, were as much a part of my upbringing as chicken for Sunday dinner. I was told, and I believed, that the meek would inherit the earth; that good does triumph; that the righteous will win; and that those who do evil are punished. The Ten Commandments were serious business. Every action in life could be neatly categorized into venial and mortal sins, and those who sinned were punished, if not immediately by God, then certainly by the Mother Superior at school.

It all made sense except if you were black, and you were young, and ambitious, and growing into intellectual and social adulthood on the eve of this country's civil rights revolution. As a young black girl, I was surrounded by constant examples of the evils of racism, of a society based on condoning inequality and oppression. In light of my grandfather's and my church's teachings, I could not understand how it was that those who did hurtful things to me and millions of my brothers and sisters were not punished, but seemingly rewarded. They had better houses and cars. They lived in better neighborhoods, went to better schools. They could beat, rape, steal from, and murder black people with seeming impunity and still call themselves Christians.

I plagued my elders with questions and challenges about how God would allow those contradictions to exist. Perhaps even more immediately, how could they allow such contradictions to exist? They tried to answer, and in my youthful impatience I dismissed all of the answers as unsatisfactory. Their responses were full of moral statements, of shoulds, and ought-tos, of visions of divine justice in a later life. It was not good enough for me. It made no sense to me. The contradictions were too raw, too outrageous to be borne. I felt as if they were somehow trying to con me, divert me from my rage as a young black woman who saw her entire future stunted and distorted by the color of her skin. I was in no mood for what I considered to be platitudes.

And then one day, in one of those white, western civilization courses, I got an assignment to read *The Prince* by Machiavelli, and it was like an explosion going off in my head. Here was a man who talked not in terms of what men ought to do morally, but in terms of what, in fact, they did do in reality. Here was a man who talked not in terms of what men should be, but of what they are, and what they are is not praiseworthy or God-like, but as he put it:

> ". . . ungrateful, fickle, simulators and deceivers, avoiders of dangers, greedy for gain. And while you work for their good, they are completely yours, offering you their blood, their property, their lives, and their sons when danger is far way. But when it comes nearer to you, they turn away. And this . . . there is such a gap between how one lives and how one ought to live that anyone who abandons what is done for what ought to be done learns his ruin rather than his preservation. For a man who wishes to make a vocation of being good at all times will come to ruin among so many who are not good."

My grandfather, the Baptist minister, had, in fact, made a vocation of being good at all times, and I had seen the price which he had paid for that as a black man in the South. I had seen countless others who kept turning the other cheek only to find themselves slapped again. It was their belief that eventually God would show their oppressors the error of their ways, and the slaps would stop.

It was Machiavelli's contention that the slaps would continue simply because force, violence, pain, and fear are effective methods of control, not ethical methods. Ethics had nothing to do with it— effective methods. Such talk was a revelation to me. Things started falling into place. The southern sheriffs with their private armies, their war canons and cattle prods, their batons and beatings, began making sense to me. The bombs that exploded killing four little black girls in a southern church one Sunday morning began making sense to me. The Klu Klux Klan cross burnings, hangings, and castrations began to make sense to me. These were not random, unchristian aberrations. They were lessons, Machiavelli told me, in effective manipulation and oppression, textbook examples of the uses of military might and violence.

I remember reading, ". . . between an armed and an unarmed man there is no comparison whatsoever. And it is not reasonable for an armed man to obey an unarmed man willingly, nor that an unarmed man should be safe among armed servants."

I thought of what might happen if the servants did try to arm themselves. These were the visions of massive bloodshed that people like Dr. Martin Luther King, Jr. worked so desperately to guard us from. I thought of that then. I think of South Africa, and the vision is equally terrifying.

I was in South Africa some months again, invited by Desmond Tutu to attend his installation as Archbishop. The South African Government had turned down four previous requests of mine for a visa to go over as a journalist. This time they approved, after some public pressure, one day before my scheduled departure. I was told that I could go, but only as a tourist, and that I could stay no longer than 7 days.

Often, parallels are made between the situation in South Africa and the situation for blacks here in the United States before the civil rights struggle, and there are indeed similarities, but there is, as a number of South Africans pointed out to me, one fundamental difference. In the United States, you had at least the pretense of law. Blacks did in fact, at least by the 20th century, have some rights as citizens, separate and unequal, but still citizens. In South Africa, blacks, in legal terms, do not exist as full human beings. They have virtually no rights. There is no pretense that the law is there to protect them. Apartheid is the foundation of their legal system, and as a black you are fair game in the most literal of senses.

For me as a black person to go voluntarily into that arena, several friends pointed out to me, was semi-suicidal, and I had no argument with them. As the plane entered South African air space, the hairs, and I know that this sounds like a melodramatic cliche—in fact it had never happened to me before—but a purely animal response, the hairs on the back of my neck went up as that plane entered South African air space. I was sensing danger. I felt more vulnerable than I ever had in my life.

If arrested or held, there was no one to call who could get me out. U.S. officials clearly had only limited influence with the South African Government, which would often go out of its way to defy U.S. requests simply to show its independence and lack of concern for American condemnation of them. If I was taken, I was conceivably lost, and that thought came back to me again and again during my time in South Africa, time I spent in black townships, in places where I was, according to their laws, not supposed to be—ducking around buildings, hiding in back rooms with black South Africans to avoid being seen by the patrols, seen and possibly taken.

It was, in a very Machiavellian sense, a pure police state, a state conceived in and controlled by force and violence. It was efficiently run. The servants knew their place and were first, and foremost, never allowed access to arms—Machiavelli's first rule.

One day, I was in a cab in Johannesburg driven by a black man. When he heard my accent, he knew immediately that I was American, and he began to talk and to question me. He wanted to know what the American people thought of the South African situation. He wanted to know if they really cared, and he wanted to know what, if anything, we might be able to do to help them win their freedom. He was, he told me, a very religious, conservative man worried about how he could continue to take care of his wife and his four children. He was against economic sanctions because, he said, he would lose his job, and there literally were no other jobs for him. Besides, he said, sanctions simply wouldn't work. The South African Government would find some way to get around them, and somehow business would go on as usual. I asked him, then, what he would do, what his solution to the problems would be, and for several moments there was silence in the cab. I thought perhaps he hadn't heard me, and I started to repeat my question, when I noticed he seemed to be looking around as if to make sure that he wasn't being watched or overheard. And then suddenly, in a very soft voice he spoke—two words—so soft that I had to crane forward to hear him and ask him to repeat them. Two words. He said, "Bomb them!"

I said, "What are you talking about? Are you really suggesting that the United States should drop bombs on South Africa?" His answer, quite simply was, yes. But I said, "That doesn't make any sense. If you're concerned about something as relatively mild as economic sanctions because of the potential harm for yourself and your family, how can you talk about dropping bombs? You and tens of thousands of other black people would die if that happened. It doesn't make any sense." "Ah, but it does to me," he said. "Sanctions would mean starving—a slow, pointless death. With bombs, death would come quickly, and I would know that my death would mean something, because it would be part of the white's defeat. I would die knowing that whatever blacks were left standing after the bombs fell, that they would be free. Why not?" he said. "Look at my life. What do I have to lose?" Then he stopped. That was it. He went back to driving, back to his life. On the surface, a quiet, uneventful life—a man ready to die.

Machiavelli warned against such men. He talked of how dangerous they can be to a prince; how vulnerable a prince can be to their sudden, totally unexpected attacks. Because, he said, "Anyone who does not fear death can harm them. But the Prince must not be too afraid of such men for they are very rare. He must only guard against inflicting serious injury on anyone who serves him." The South Africans might do well to read Machiavelli's advice, for desperation is apparently making such men less and less rare.

That cab driver forced me to face the reality of violence brought to its ultimate conclusion, a man so determined to destroy his enemy that he would accept his own destruction as the price. The end result? Potential nothingness, the ashes of a society—a picture I could not accept. And intellectually, emotionally, I turned away from it, continuing the search for other peaceful, non-violent solutions, but it was a picture that the driver not only accepted, but actively painted.

My inability to accept it taught me some things about myself at that moment, some things about what horrors I am willing to accept, and what I cannot even bear to contemplate about the boundaries, if any, to my commitments, about how far I am willing to go for what I believe in. They are deeply troubling questions that I continue to answer as I change, and grow, and am challenged in my life.

Machiavelli has helped that process in me for many years; forcing me to carry my thinking and my feelings about morality, about mankind, about values, to their ultimate conclusions; forcing me to face his terrible truths and see when and if I flinched, when and if I turned away; to see what I really believed in. Do I, for instance, really believe that men are inherently evil, that they cannot be moved to struggle for a cause simply because it is right or just, but instead can only be moved by self-interest. Do I really believe "...that all armed prophets were victorious, and the unarmed came to ruin? That people are fickle by nature, and it is simple to convince them of something, but difficult to hold them in that conviction, that therefore, affairs should be managed in such a way that when they no longer believe, they can be made to believe by force." Do I really believe the full and fully evil picture of life and mankind drawn by Machiavelli? And the answer is no.

There are parts of it that ring true, parts of it that make a terrible, unavoidable sense, but do I accept it all in whole cloth? No. What Machiavelli has continually forced me to do is constantly to re-examine and question what my beliefs are, to put daily reality through his filter and really see the essence that comes through. And what I found is that, as often as not, the essence is a more positive affirmation of man- and womankind, of the strength, beauty, kindness, and creativity that we are capable of.

I find that the faith my grandfather tried to instill in me is still there, but it is tempered and strengthened by being forged in Machiavelli's fires. I have a stronger belief in what I and others can accomplish, but Machiavelli has removed a certain naivete, has given me a painful sense of how tough the journey will be, and what circuitous tactics may be necessary to get where I want to go, to advance the causes that I believe in, to wring all from life that I can.

For women, for instance, swimming in professional waters once charted only by men, Machiavelli has quite a few lessons to share, particularly about something women have had little access to—power. Women, on the whole, have been socialized to be nurturers, to weigh their own worth by how much they are loved, by how much others approve of them.

In recent years, tens of thousands of women have been discovering that that is not a very appropriate approach to survival in the corporate world. As their heads bump hard against the so-called glass ceiling, and their professional rise inexplicably stops, they can begin to run into certain unspoken vestiges of double standards that still linger in our society. They might discover, for instance, that forcefulness and aggressiveness are considered not only appropriate but critical, for a man doing certain jobs, but similar behavior on the part of a woman in the same job is often considered totally inappropriate, that she is too tough. To use one of the nicer terms often aimed at her, that she is a "bitch" or even, "an aggressive, power hungry bitch."

As Barbara Walters points out, when Mike Wallace asks a tough question, he's just doing his job. When she asks the same question, she's out of line, way out of line, and she gets a lot of flack.

And Machiavelli tells modern women that they have had to grapple with this realization, that they are caught in a catch-22, that sometimes the very qualities that allow them to do their jobs well are, in fact, the same qualities that may keep them from being approved of, of being liked, of being loved by those around them, and that at some point they may have to make a very, very difficult choice. Machiavelli tells them that . . .

> "From this arises an argument. Whether it is better to be loved than to be feared, or the contrary. I reply that one should like to be both one and the other, but since it is difficult to join them together, it is much safer to be feared than to be loved when one of the two must be lacking."

He goes on to explain that men are. . .

> ". . . less hesitant about harming someone who makes himself loved than one who makes himself feared, because love is held together by a chain of obligation which, since men are a sorry lot, is broken on every occasion in which their own self-interest is concerned. But fear is held together by a dread of punishment which will never abandon you."

It is a problem faced by the few women who have taken on the leadership not only of companies but countries as well—how to balance the nurturer role with the authority role. Most women struck some form of compromise—Indira Ghandi, Golda Meier, for instance. Others, like Corizon Aquino, are finding the compromise a difficult one at best, as her own government officials accuse her of not being tough enough, decisive enough, male enough to run the country. And then, of course, there's Margaret Thatcher—one of the few women leaders seemingly untroubled by those kinds of conflicts. She has opted whole hog for the authority figure role, the steely-eyed wielder of power, and no matter what various people might think of her politics, she seems to have won the sometimes grudging respect of most of her countrymen. As one British bartender put it to me in a London pub, "She thinks and acts like a man. You hardly think of her as a woman now, do you?"

Margaret Thatcher clearly understands and does not shrink away from the uses and the costs of power. She probably could have given

Machiavelli lessons on leadership. Those lessons are very much a part of our modern American corporate structure.

Browse through a book store section on business management, and you will find a host of books which easily could have been written by Machiavelli himself, from *Winning Through Intimidation* to *Swim with the Sharks Without Being Eaten Alive!*

The worlds they depict are largely amoral jungles where the only value is beating the competition, and the only measure of your worth is monetary. It is a mean, cruel place where the Ivan Boeskys of the world are the symbols of success until they commit the cardinal sin—not lying or cheating, but getting caught lying or cheating.

As Machiavelli pointed out, "A Prince never lacks legitimate reasons to break his promises." Of this, one could cite an endless number of modern examples to show how many pacts, how many promises have been made null and void because of the infidelity of princes. "But it is necessary," he says, "to know how to disguise this nature well and to be a great hypocrite and liar."

In a Machiavellian world where so many people assume that their leaders are, in fact, hypocrites and liars, is it a coincidence that the two men running for president present themselves primarily not as visionaries and charismatic leaders, as people whom we really need to lead in terms of their philosophies of life, but instead present themselves as good managers, tacticians? Is it a coincidence that the polls show the main problem for many voters is that they don't really have a sense of what the candidates do believe in, what their values are? Some suggest that it is not coincidental at all, that our candidates reflect our own confusion as a society, that we no longer know what we believe in, that Watergate destroyed our faith in government. The Jimmy Bakkers and the Jimmy Swaggerts of the world tainted our expectations of some of our representatives of the church. And the All-American nuclear family of mom, dad, and 2.2 children, virtually no longer exists. The simple beliefs and values don't seem to work any more. They've been thrown out, and along with them, the moral imperatives that used to guide us and give us a framework within which to conduct our lives. We are reduced to floundering in an environment, some would say a Machiavellian environment, where the means do justify the end.

That is certainly true for an alarming number of our children, particularly those surrounded by poverty and drugs. Some of them really do not have problems with the notion of killing as an appropriate means to the end of something as simple as a stereo. They see themselves as so lacking in value that their lives are worth no more than a pair of designer jeans or a hit of PCP. They look at the leaders of government and industry in this country through eyes made old by cynicism, expecting lies, expecting cheating, expecting drug and alcohol abuse, expecting hypocrisy, expecting Machiavelli's world. And too often, unfortunately, they get it!

And my industry doesn't help. The television camera, by its very nature, almost inevitably distorts reality. What we present to tens of millions of Americans every night are fragmented segments of a world, seemingly inhabited by a disproportionately high number of prostitutes, drug dealers, police, private detectives, and lawyers. It is an extremely violent world where disputes are settled mainly by force.

Studies have found that people who watch television fairly frequently come to have two characteristics. They believe that the world is much more violent than it really is, and they become largely immune to, untouched by the violence that they see. They accept it, as Machiavelli accepted it, as the natural order of things.

Television's technical capabilities have reached the point where we can create virtually any illusion for you to watch. We can place people who are sitting in a television studio virtually anywhere in the world. Anchor people pop up in the middle of launch pads. Actors seemingly walk through doors. Animals disappear. Everything becomes an illusion, and you can never be sure that what you are actually seeing is really there, that you can really believe in it, whether it is a situation or a politician.

What was it Machiavelli said? "Everyone sees what you seem to be. Few perceive what you are."

Machiavelli's world exists very much behind the cameras also. TV broadcasting is not particularly glamorous. It is a tough, often very mean, business. The network news divisions in recent months have been devastated by major layoffs, and the integrity of the product that they produce has been tarnished by a slew of revealing new books on the seamy, sometimes cruel, underbelly of the business.

I remember the day I had just one glimpse too many of that underbelly, and I decided to leave my job as a network correspondent. I have functioned for some time in a milieu where Machiavelli's management techniques seemed to have full rein at the network—the studied hypocrisies, the use of fear to intimidate and manipulate reporters, the small cruelties carefully inflicted. It was an atmosphere where kindness was dismissed as weakness; where the competitive fighter instinct was encouraged not only against one's journalistic competitors, but against each other. It could make you a damned good reporter, but it could also make you a pretty rotten human being.

I have been relatively unscathed by it. I was a small fish in a very large pond. I was hardly a worthwhile target, simply one of the drones; but I was surrounded by others who had been there much longer, who bore the marks that working in that kind of insecure, unfeeling environment can leave on you. I had not understood much of what I had seen. The management gestures often seemed arbitrary in their harshness.

But one day as I sat at my desk, I overheard a conversation, a heated conversation, at the desk next to mine, a conversation between a veteran, respected correspondent and his manager, his supervisor. The correspondent was asking for a day off, just asking for a day off, to attend his son's high school graduation. He had been working for 32 days straight covering a series of hearings on The Hill. There was no emergency.

He went to management to ask them what to do, to ask them to do that very thing. They said no. No justification, just no. I listened to the correspondent who had given 20 years of his life to that organization go from reasoned arguments to desperate pleas, trying to explain the urgency of the matter, how important it was to his son, how he'd missed his son's grade school graduation because he was out of town on a story, how much it would mean to his family, how after all these years couldn't they at least . . . and it went on and on, painful minute after painful minute, as the manager sat there quite calmly simply saying, "No. Sorry, we'd like to. But, no, we just can't spare you."

Eventually, I got up and left. I went to another room. I was embarrassed for the correspondent. I was angered at the company's humiliation of him. And as I fumed, part of the exchange came back to me, and something clicked in place. The manager had kept saying, at various times during his refusal, "Now, don't take this personally." And, in fact, I began to realize that he was right. This was not a personal attack against this correspondent. This was an exercise in management technique, in control and manipulation, the kind of manipulation Machiavelli had so carefully outlined 400 years earlier, the kind of manipulation outlined in business management books on our bookstore shelves right now. That realization made it easier for me to understand, but not to accept. I resigned the next day, and I knew that my next job would have to be in an environment where I would be less vulnerable to that kind of manipulation, that I would have to figure out how to be a bigger fish in a small pond.

All of this, I know, sounds terribly negative, all of these lessons learned from Machiavelli, the seemingly uniformly evil and depressing world view. But in the final analysis, what I have gotten from Machiavelli is very positive.

He helped me to know the enemy within and without, to recognize evil when I see it and not to shrink away from it. He also helped me to recognize that there are patterns to evil behavior, patterns that if pinpointed and plotted, can be countered and blocked for positive, rather than negative, goals. Machiavelli, to my mind, is in some ways a romantic and fundamentally an optimist.

As you go back to read and reread sections of *The Prince*, what emerges is a man who believes, for instance, that man can control his fate, that he need not lie down and simply accept the miseries of life, that he as an individual has the power to bring about change. This section, for instance,

> "It is not unknown to me that many have held, and still hold, the opinion that the things of this world are in a manner controlled by Fortune and by God; that men with their wisdom cannot control them, and on the contrary that men can have no remedy whatsoever for them. And for this reason, they might judge that they need not sweat much over such matters, but let them be governed by fate."

He goes on,

> "Sometimes, as I think about these things, I am inclined to their opinion to a certain extent. Nevertheless, in order that our free will not be extinguished, I judge it to be true that Fortune is the arbiter of one half of our actions, but that she still leaves the control of the other half, or almost that, to us."

Those are the words of a man who is a fighter. Those are the kinds of words that can bring solace and support to people everywhere who are struggling against oppression, struggling against the accepted wisdom that their misery is somehow destined, ordered by Fate, or by an unforgiving God—destined and therefore unchangeable. Those are the kinds of words that that taxi driver in South Africa might be willing to hear.

If you reread Machiavelli, what emerges is a man who believes that power must be used to some extent for the benefit of the masses; that a good or skillful leader cannot be a cruel tyrant for, as he says, "It cannot be skill to kill one's fellow citizens, to betray friends, to be without faith, without mercy, without religion. By these means, one can acquire power, but not glory."

What emerges is a man for whom, contrary to general belief, power is not in and of itself an acceptable end, a man who makes clear distinctions about how that power should be used. What emerges is, perhaps, a man convinced that by writing a how-to primer for tyrants he could help others guard against tyranny. What emerges is a man desperately in love with his country, angry at the inept, immoral leadership that has so harmed its people, a man whose final words conjure up images of those in our own society who speak so nostalgically for the days of our own country's political Camelot—the Kennedy years—when our new, young prince seemed single-handedly destined to bring our country into a new, energetic, enlightened era.

As a major anniversary of John Kennedy's death approaches this November, we will hear more of that nostalgia, a yearning to somehow recreate what is past. Many of those who yearn are dismissed as foolhardy romantics. Think of them, and then listen to the closing sentences of this man, Machiavelli, in *The Prince* who supposedly epitomizes the depths of political cynicism. Listen to him as he calls for the emergence of a new leader for his beloved Italy, the longing as he pleads for a skillful and prudent prince whose rule will bring him honor and bring the people good. Listen to the almost breathless enthusiasm with which he cries out for a new redeemer for his country. He says,

> "Nor, can I express with what love he will be received in all those provinces that have suffered through these foreign floods, with what compassion, with what tears. What doors will be closed to him? Which people will deny him obedience? What jealousy depose him? What Italian would deny him homage? This barbarian dominion stinks to everyone. Therefore, may your illustrious house take up this mission with that spirit and with that hope in which just undertakings are begun, so that under your banner this country may be ennobled, and under your guidance those words of Petrarch may come true: 'Discipline over rage will take up arms, and the battle will be short, for ancient valor in Italian hearts is not yet dead.'"

The words of a cynic? I think not. More so, the words of someone perhaps a little like me, painfully skeptical, but wanting to believe that the good guys will win in the end. Thank you.

Q. *Is it possible as a journalist to be your own person and still report the news objectively?*

RENÉE POUSSAINT: I think that that's probably one of the more fundamental issues of the business as a matter of fact. When I first started studying journalism and studying the business, I was told that as a reporter my role was to be objective. Now, I asked what that meant, and I was told that it meant that you had no opinion about the story that you were doing. I find that difficult. It's a kind of double-edged sword situation. No matter what you say, you can raise an eyebrow while Bush is talking, and every Republican in Washington will be on the phone. They will see that as a comment. You can move the right side of your mouth down while Dukakis speaks, and every Democrat will be on the phone saying that you made a statement about Dukakis.

So, I think we bend over backwards sometimes to appear to be balanced and fair to both sides, and therefore end up saying nothing of worth. We fill up a lot of time, but we say nothing of worth, and try and give basically platitudes.

I understand; struggling with the issue of objectivity has been one of the most difficult things for me in this business. It is very difficult, and it has been very difficult for me, for instance, to be objective about the South Africa story. It has been very difficult for me . . . at one stage I was sent out to cover the growth of the Klu Klux Klan in Illinois. Now, standing there interviewing the Grand Kleegle was not exactly something that I felt distanced from.

But one of the things that I came to understand also was how important it was to try and be fair with viewers and not insert yourself into a story. The story that taught me the most about that was a story that had to do with the rape of a child, and this was in Chicago. And I remember when I first got into this business, and I walked into the news director's office where I was applying for this job. I said to him, "Don't hire me if you want somebody who can go and stick a microphone in the face of a grieving mother who has just lost her child, or a grieving wife who has just lost her husband in some violent incident and say, 'How do you feel?' I can't do that. I told him, "I can't do that, so don't hire me if that's what you want." And he said, "Oh, no. We don't do that sort of thing here. No, no, no. That's *National Enquirer* stuff. We are a serious television station." And that lasted for about 4 months. One day, I was out on a story with a crew in a car, and the word came over our crew radio that they wanted me to head over to try and interview the mother of a child who had been abducted, had been missing for 4 days—a 10-year-old girl—who had just been found crawling on a street. She had been held in a warehouse by a guy for 4 days and raped numerous times, and cut at least 40 times over her body. She was closer to death than being alive. She had been taken to the hospital, and my news director wanted me to go interview the mother! And I went back to the station, and we had what you would call a knock-down-drag-out fight. I just refused to do it. I couldn't do it. And he was giving me stuff about being objective about the story. "What are you getting so emotional about, Renée? Just be objective about the story!" Well, I couldn't be, so I resigned. I stormed out of there. I slammed the door. I was on my way; I didn't know where. I was leaving.

Well, one of the cameramen—very Machiavellian—came up to me, and he said, "Renée, wait a minute. Wait! Wait! You don't have to go out and resign over this. Think about it. Plan. Think. You go to the woman's house to get the interview. She's not going to be home, Renée. She's going to be at the hospital with her child. The child is in intensive care. The mother is going to be sequestered. You're not going to be able to get to her, but you're going to be able to say, 'I tried.' You'll still have your job. You won't have to do the interview. Stop being so emotional about it." So I said, "Okay. All right. That seems reasonable to me."

So we went to the mother's house, a little run-down house, went up, banged on the door. Not only was Mom home, Mom was home dressed in her Sunday best waiting for the media to show up. She had been poor all of her life. She had been plagued by health problems all of her life. She had too many children, and not enough money, and nobody had ever paid any attention to her, and this was her chance to shine! She sat there with two of her sons by her side and beamed as the camera lights went on, and I sat there interviewing her, and I realized half way through that interview that I was enraged. I was so angry with that woman I could barely talk to her. I wanted to say, "What the Hell are you doing here? Why aren't you with your child? She's dying in a hospital. What the Hell are you doing here talking to me?"

And I didn't do that, but I got through the interview, and I went back to the station to put the story together, and I wrote the story ten times. It was the hardest story that I've ever had to write, because every time I wrote it my rage was in that story. I was writing a story saying to the viewers, "I want you to disapprove of this woman the way I disapprove of this woman. She has no right to do this! She has no right to behave this way."

And I talked it over with another correspondent who was a very good friend of mine, and he said, "Yea. This is the toughest thing you have to do, because you do get emotionally drawn into stories. You do want to say to people, 'This makes no sense. This guy's lyin' his head off.' But you don't have the right to do that. You are there to give information. You are there to give, hopefully, enough information so people can form their own judgments."

I had no right to judge that woman, certainly not as a professional. As a human being, I couldn't help it, but as a professional it was up to the viewers to make up their own mind. And, I made myself, after a while, and I'm still going through it, walk in her shoes, to try to understand her life, which I can't really do. But it was a good lesson for me to go through.

And every single time I am in a position where I feel strongly about something, but I am forced to be "objective," I think of that woman, and I think of that story, and I try to cleanse the me from the story that I write and present. And those are the kinds of scripts and the kinds of stories I'll hand to a colleague and I'll say, "Read that and tell me if my value judgments are in there;" and if they are, I've got to start all over again, because I don't think it's fair. I don't want other journalists doing it to me about stories that they cover, and I don't think I have the right to do it to anybody else.

So, long answer, because it is one of the most troubling questions about our business, the issue of objectivity. I don't know how to maintain it very well lots of times. And particularly since, as I said, when I leave here I'm going to do a live special on drug abuse, a lot of it will have to do with children. I'm not objective about that. It's very, very difficult, but that's part of the challenge of the business.

Howard J. Gray, S.J.

ON

The Spiritual Exercises of St. Ignatius Loyola

Inspired and composed between 1522 and 1548, the text of the *Spiritual Exercises* of St. Ignatius Loyola constitutes the fundamental orientation for Jesuit apostolic vision and the authentic strategies necessary to implement it.[1] It is true that the Constitutions of the Society of Jesus detail the corporate life of the membership. It is also true that subsequent legislative bodies called General Congregations have brought Jesuit corporate life into harmony with cultural and social changes and emerging apostolic needs. Nonetheless, the Constitutions of the Society of Jesus and the decrees of the General Congregations derive their power to inspire action and to guide practical decisions for genuine service from the vision and strategy of the *Spiritual Exercises*.

Consequently, in a symposium sponsored by a university itself sponsored by the Society of Jesus, it is appropriate that someone attend to this important Jesuit text. I am honored to be that person. Before I outline my procedure, allow me to communicate a *caveat*. While I have emphasized the indebtedness which Jesuits have to the *Spiritual Exercises* of St. Ignatius Loyola, I do not want to neglect the wider Christian community which also has found in this text similar apostolic vision and strategy. While the heart of Jesuit life, the *Spiritual Exercises* are not exclusively its property. The *Spiritual Exercises* belong to the entire human community and, indeed, have been the object of scrutiny by believers, non-Catholics, and atheists. Therefore, while I shall discuss the significance of the Exercises as a Jesuit, I acknowledge the interest and even affection which non-Jesuits have extended to this text.

I would like to discuss three aspects of the *Spiritual Exercises*: their vision, their strategy, and their enduring significance for the Christian humanist. However, before I develop these three topics, I want to say something about the title and the external structure of the *Spiritual Exercises*.

The word "spiritual" means something profoundly real for Ignatius Loyola.[2] To understand the term in its Ignatian context, one must understand the significance of the closing exercise of the entire *Spiritual Exercises*, the Contemplation to attain Divine Love.[3] In this final, and climactic, exercise, Ignatius proposes to the person who has spent close to thirty days in intense prayer and reflection that he or she see life as constituted by two realities: the action of God in creation and the freedom of the human person to accept that divine action as a personal gift of love. "Spiritual" symbolizes the power of divine love to lead human freedom into partnership with God, accepting God's desires to effect enduring good.

The term "exercises" indicates both the total experience of prayer, reflection, and examination which constitute the thirty days of solitude and the specific methods which the retreatant uses to pray, to reflect, and to examine his or her life. Ignatius puts it this way:

> By this name of Spiritual Exercises is meant every way of examining one's conscience, of meditating, of contemplating, of praying vocally and mentally, and of performing other spiritual actions, as will be said later. For as strolling, walking and running are bodily exercises, so every way of preparing and disposing the soul to rid itself of all the disordered tendencies, and, after it is rid, to seek and find the Divine Will as to the management of one's life for the salvation of the soul is called a Spiritual Exercise.[4]

My second preliminary consideration concerns the external structure of the text of the *Spiritual Exercises*. Briefly put, the text is a set of ascetical proposals, prayer forms, and guidelines to help the director of the experience of the *Spiritual Exercises* lead another Christian through the thirty days of retreat. The dominant external structure is a set of prayer forms and subject matter under the headings: "weeks." There are four "weeks" in the *Spiritual Exercises*. These "weeks" signify less a chronological sequence than a psychoreligious development based on Christian revelation. The major topics for each week are: *Week One*: the loved sinner is called to reorient his or her freedom toward the good; *Week Two*: the person and methodology of Jesus Christ as the embodiment of human freedom oriented toward the good are offered for imitation; *Week Three*: the mystery of suffering and the cost of Christian discipleship—both exemplified in the Death of Jesus—confirm or strengthen the resolve to live in the likeness of Christ's life; and *Week Four*: the triumph of human freedom is exemplified in the exaltation of Jesus by the Father, which both affirms the power of fidelity and the promise of similar triumph to the faithful Christian.

The *Exercises* are a text to help the director lead a serious Christian to the radical dedication to live his or her life in the conscious imitation of Jesus Christ. This "imitation" of Christ is neither a mimicking of the external details of Christ's historical existence nor a simply moral adherence to the tenets of Christ's teaching; rather Ignatian imitation is first an openness toward and then a readiness to make the vision and strategy of Jesus one's own way of being human.

These preliminary considerations bring me to the body of my presentation. As a Jesuit educator and administrator whose professional life has been centered on Jesuit and priestly formation and the internal government of the Jesuit order, I have had to live closely with the *Spiritual Exercises* less as a text than as the constitutive element in helping young Jesuits to understand their vocations and to give direction to their energies and talents. If there is such a thing as a Jesuit theology, it will be found in the *Spiritual Exercises*. Finally, the *Spiritual Exercises* have been for me a heuristic structure for my own apostolic work, providing me with a vision and a strategy to be a Christian and a Jesuit in a highly secularized and complex age. It is this vision and strategy which I shall emphasize, concluding with some reflections on the enduring humanistic values inherent in the *Spiritual Exercises*.

VISION OF THE SPIRITUAL EXERCISES

Vision stands for the contemplative orientation of the imagination, affections, and energies of the human person toward some dominant value. Ignatius defines this vision as the *id quod volo*, the fundamental desires which structure one's prayer and which engage one's future directions. As a structure for prayer and a future direction, the vision of the *Spiritual Exercises* touches both the "now" of the solitude of the thirty-day retreat and the "then" of the future life of the one undergoing the experience of the *Exercises*. The content of that vision, i.e., the "now" and "then" of the various movements in the Exercises, is well summarized in the climatic reflection of the *Spiritual Exercises*, the Contemplation to attain Divine Love.[5]

There are four movements in this climatic exercise: God gives; God dwells in God's creation; God labors within creation to bring it to its perfection; and God guides creation to God's selfhood as both the source and the fulfillment of creation. Each of these four movements prompts a response from the person undergoing the experience of the *Spiritual Exercises*:

> Take, O Lord, and receive all my liberty, my memory, my intellect, and all my will—all that I have or possess Thou gavest all to me: to Thee, Lord, I return it! All is Thine, dispose of it according to all Thy will. Give me only Thy love and grace, for this is enough for me (#234).

The vision of the first movement, God's donation in creation, recapitulates the experience of the First Week of the *Exercises*, the initial psychoreligious reality of Christian life, God is good and giving. The primary good which God donates is creation, life in all its richness offered to the human person in the symbol of partnership dramatized in Genesis, chapters 1 and 2. However, for Ignatius that initial partnership between God as good and giving and the human as free to accept that good was ruptured by sin. For Ignatius sin is real and destructive; but sin is primarily personal. The movement of the First Week is not a history observed but a history renewed in the personal culpability of the one making the *Exercises*, who experiences within the history of sin his or her own folly and weakness. Yet this realization of one's own role in the abuse of the good given in creation is, for Ignatius, a moment of turning not to despair but to new hope. The vision of sinfulness is also the vision of mercy, for to see oneself as needing redemption is to be redeemed.

Thus the gifts given are not only specific incidents where one can recount people, places, times, and talents which are life-affirming, but the overall direction of all good.

Gratitude for the gifts acknowledged and gratitude for repentance over the gifts abused mark both the First Week and the recapitulation of that week in the first movement of the Contemplation to attain Divine Love.

The response to the profound personal realization that God does not withdraw himself is to give to God one's own radical good, that is, one's freedom. For Ignatius Loyola, to be human is to be the creature capable of freedom. This freedom is not just the absence of physical, psychological, or moral impositions but rather Christian freedom as described in Galatians 5:1, 13-15:

> Christ set us free, to be free people . . . You, my friends, were called to be free people; Only do not turn your freedom into license for your lower nature, but be servants to one another in

love. For the whole law can be summed up in a single commandment: 'Love your neighbors as yourself.'

This is a freedom not only from something, sin, but a freedom toward something, love.

The second point of the Contemplation to attain Divine Love corresponds to the Second Week of the *Spiritual Exercises*. This second point invites the retreatant to see God as dwelling within creation. This indwelling God is preeminently found in Christ, the one who came "to dwell among us" (John 1:14). The central concern of the Second Week of the *Exercises* is the person and mission of Jesus Christ. The prayer of the Second Week becomes increasingly intersubjective as the retreatant identifies through his or her humanity with the humanity of Jesus. In Christ's historical restrictions, one sees one's own; in Christ's call, one hears one's own; in Christ's weariness, exultations, capacity for friendship and agony of rejection, struggle for clarity, and desire to be faithful to his best moments, one recognizes one's own emerging humanity. The ennobling of humanness for the Christian is intimately related to the Incarnation, the mystery of the Word taking flesh. For Ignatius, the essential understanding of the Incarnation is the choice of Jesus to be both human and good. In the freedom of Christ, Ignatius perceives the locale for Christian discipleship: to choose to be human and to choose to do the good as did Christ.

The response of the retreatant to this second point of the Contemplation to attain Divine Love as a recapitulation of Week Two of the *Exercises* is once more the Suscipe, "Take, Lord, and receive my liberty . . ." This second donation of the self is more specific than the first. Now the man or woman who has undergone the experience of the *Spiritual Exercises* knows himself or herself as one pledged to the humanity of Jesus Christ. By that, I mean two realities: (1) the personal realization that the best hermeneutic for understanding the revelation found in Christ is one's own humanity, and, paradoxically, (2) the best hermeneutic for understanding the revelation found in myself is Christ's humanity. This reciprocity is important for Ignatius and for the *Exercises*. If the prayer and grace of the Second Week are effective, then the one making the *Spiritual Exercises* has come to a personal realization of what friendship means. For Ignatius, the bonding of friendship is a bonding of freedoms to achieve the good.

The third point of the Contemplation to attain Divine Love focuses on God laboring within creation, echoing in the vocabulary of this presentation one of the chief notions of Week Three of the *Exercises*, that is, the labor of Christ in his Passion and Death and the labor of the retreatant in the painful concentration on the significance of human suffering represented in Jesus and in the acceptance of the hard truth that if one accepts humanity in Jesus Christ, then one accepts, as well, the cost of such discipleship. This laboring God in the third point of the Contemplation to attain Divine Love is not only Christ suffering but also the Father suffering, who "loved the world so much that he gave his only Son" (John 3:16). The *pati humana* is also the *pati divina*, i.e., the Christ suffering in himself and as representative of all suffering humanity is also God for Ignatius, a God concealing himself in the agony of Jesus. For the chalice offered Jesus in the Garden was the chalice of God's vulnerability, a love sustained in its offering even in the face of rejection.

The third repetition of the *Suscipe* symbolizes a still more profound acceptance of God's way, of God's vision. The freedom to choose to love even in pain, in anguish, and even in rejection is at the core of Christian asceticism and Christian service. The Christian cannot find enemies. The Christian can only find, as did Christ and as does the God Christ represents, those to love through forgiveness to friendship. To accept this radical vulnerability is to accept the consequences of discipleship. This acceptance is the finality of the Week Three of the *Spiritual Exercises*.

Finally, the Contemplation to attain Divine Love progresses to a consideration of God redirecting all creation to Himself, recapitulating for the retreatant the movement of Week Four of the *Spiritual Exercises*. In Week Four the mystery of Christ's Resurrection and Ascension represent two realities for one making the *Exercises*: (1) that Christ in the Spirit continues to abide in his disciples as a counselor and (2) that the one who has pledged himself or herself to full discipleship can find joy and peace in believing and hoping in the power of God to bring life to death, meaning to suffering, and fulfillment in the Kingdom out of the struggle against evil.

The fourth repetition of the *Suscipe*, "Take, Lord, and receive all my liberty . . .," is yet a more profound donation than the three which have preceded it. The ultimate Christian self-donation is to bring one's commitment to life and to joy by becoming committed to effect God's design for a world more faithful and more just.

To persevere in living a committed Christian life of professional competence and apostolic dedication in an increasingly secularized society demands a vision at once realistically sensitive to seeing the reality of evil and the attack on the good, and yet also prophetically enlightened to seeing the hope of the Kingdom of God in Christ as an event capable of realization. For me, the contemplation to attain Divine Love recapitulates this vision of reality and prophecy, summoning at once to conversion from fear or cynicism in the face of so much war, too much starvation, and too deeply embedded self-interest, and to a dedication to the only task worthy of human effort: establishing peace, justice, wisdom, and, especially, love.

However, a vision without strategy would become frustrating. If the *Spiritual Exercises* summon one to see, they also summon one to act. This is the second consideration I wish to explore: the strategy of the *Spiritual Exercises*.

THE STRATEGY OF THE SPIRITUAL EXERCISES

The techniques of the *Spiritual Exercises* have received a great deal of attention: e.g., its prayer forms, the psychological structures of the various weeks, the various suggestions for maintaining an atmosphere at once reflective yet conducive to the choice of a state of life or career in harmony with one's graces, temperament, and talents.[6] I am not talking about these techniques but rather about the strategy of the *Spiritual Exercises*. What is the distinction?

Technique looks to the immediate implementation of an action. For example, Ignatius suggests that the one making the *Exercises* darken the room used for prayer while reflecting on the tough reality of sin in Week One (#79). Another example of technique is Ignatius' injunction against anticipating a future prayer subject, e.g., discipleship, when one is in another rhythm of the *Exercises*, e.g. Week One (e.g., #78, #127, #206). Obviously, these kinds of directives are means to attain a specific end within the context of the *Exercises*.

Strategy, on the other hand, looks toward those abiding dispositions and methodologies which sustain a value. In the *Spiritual Exercises* Ignatius structures three key strategies which, while operational within the *Exercises*, are also meant to be enduring ways to keep the fourfold vision of God's love and human response—summarized in the prayer of the Contemplation to attain Divine Love—alive. These Ignatian strategies are: the use of solitude, the support of companionship, and Christian choice as the exercise of genuine freedom. Let me take up each of these.

The text of the *Spiritual Exercises* emphasizes the personal and individual experience of the fourfold vision I have explored. This emphasis on the personal and the individual is a strategy found in a long history of discovering God in the reality of oneself. Ignatius does not eschew social influences; indeed, he is acutely sensitive to these (e.g., #102, ##136-147, ##149-156). However, what Ignatius asks from the one making the full *Spiritual Exercises* is that he or she be generous and reverent (#3, #5) in finding God's leadership in his or her life. This divine leadership accommodates itself to the uniqueness of the individual; and solitude is a unique context in which to discover one's selfhood before God. Ignatius does not equate solitude with simply "being alone." Rather, it is being alone with one's values, one's desires, hopes, and history. It is not empty space but simple space. It is human consciousness before its deepest reality. Ignatius asks the one who leaves the experience of the *Spiritual Exercises* to abide beyond that thirty-day event with his or her values.

Complementary to the strategy of solitude for Ignatius is the strategy of companionship. While one must, for Ignatius, undergo his or her experience and not someone else's (##2 and 15), that experience needs authenticity, the testing of community (##6, 7, 8, 9, and, especially, 10, 12-14, 16-18). The director of the *Spiritual Exercises* is both a symbol of Christian companionship and the occasion for that companionship. The director is guide, counselor, and educator, not in his or her own name but in the name of all who hear the Christian tradition, the community of faith. Moreover, the text of the *Spiritual Exercises* invites the retreatant to view himself or herself as part of human history and, therefore, involved in human destiny (e.g., ##55-61; 101-109; 237). For Ignatius, to be alone in authentic relationship to one's values leads to the ability to donate oneself to reality—human, historical, and personal. For, on the one hand, if solitude is absent, then one risks being formed by opinion, appetite, or expediency but not by values. On the other hand, if companionship is absent, one risks imposing solely personal experience on others and calling that experience "shared values." But when both solitude and companionship are maintained, one achieves a psychoreligious balance in the way he or she relates to personal and to social reality. In the *Spiritual Exercises*, the retreatant learns an abiding method for being both responsible to oneself and accountable to one's times and fellow human beings.

Finally, Ignatius offers a third major strategy, that of the exercise of freedom by choosing in an explicitly Christian context. Freedom, as I noted earlier, is key for Ignatius. That freedom realizes itself in choice, the power to make specific decisions about how one will relate to his or her values in community. Both freedom, as a Christian power, and choice, as a Christian decision, need context.[7] The context for Ignatius is solitude and companionship, preeminently companionship with Christ in prayer. The prayer of the *Spiritual Exercises* is a prayer which asks to be with Christ who chose the leadership of God as his Father. Ignatius believes that the reverent and generous Christian can choose in the likeness of Christ to lay down his or her life in the service of the human family. Ultimately, Ignatian choice—be it to build a school, to send men to a Third World project, to confront a specific social problem—demands the solitude of personal integrity before God, and challenges us to give concreteness to that choice through love, an effective desire to do good to others.

The *Spiritual Exercises* come to life only by experiencing them, and not just in their reading. For me to talk about them has meant that I try to approximate the experience—to delineate affectively their vision and their strategy. However, the *Exercises*, as vision and strategy, say something beyond the immediate experience of the actual thirty-day retreat. They say something, too, of abiding humanistic value.

THE ABIDING HUMANISTIC VALUE OF THE SPIRITUAL EXERCISES

No Jesuit has a problem assuming the abiding value of a text which grounds his vocation and its development. Such a text unites him to the great men of his order, past and present, and continues to provide both vision and strategy to others dedicated to sustained Christian influence and service. Nonetheless, the question arises, especially in an age of increasing secularity and religious indifference, whether, as text and as experience, the *Spiritual Exercises* speak to Americans of realities we can cherish enough to hand on to succeeding generations. I believe that the *Exercises* do represent three important realities for those engaged in the continuing education and formation of the American mind and heart: (1) the need to experience a tradition, (2) the meaning and experience of love, and (3) the call to social ecology.

Tradition stands for the cherished realities which generations pass to one another: our art, music, and literature, our science and philosophy, our system of government. In an age of immediacies and swiftly emerging and declining fads, tradition has fallen on hard times, appearing to some as irrelevant or to others as the property of the elite. The *Spiritual Exercises* of Ignatius Loyola presume that the Judaeo-Christian past affects the present. They demand investment of time, energy, and psychological attention. This personal investment makes the retreatant an integral part of tradition through personal commitment to its values. The prayer of the *Spiritual Exercises* is the instrument whereby the retreatant becomes, through grace, attuned to the values of Christian life. This prayer leads to a choice which determines how one will live his or her private and public life as a

Christian. Whatever our beliefs, we have invested ourselves in tradition, in the good of the past continuing to influence the present. A university like Georgetown believes that good teaching means inviting students to live, to experience the deepest realities of art, literature, history, philosophy, and the sciences as their own. Tradition is more than acceptance of what has been; it is living what has been proved to be worthwhile. That kind of personal contact and personal assimilation of one's tradition frees a man or woman to discriminate what within the contemporary genuinely gives life and hope and truth. In an age when education can too frequently be reduced to how to make a living, the *Spiritual Exercises* represent those great texts and profound experiences which challenge a man or woman to ask first, what is the meaning one should take from life. Tradition enables us to locate ourselves and our times so that we can choose with an awareness of what is truly enduring in the human spirit.

Second, the *Spiritual Exercises* explore and define the meaning of love and prompt the retreatant to experience himself or herself as both loved and capable of loving. I am assuming a general understanding of love as both benevolence toward others and the affection which follows from this or prompts it. The *Spiritual Exercises* presume both God's love for humans and the capacity of the one involved in the experience of the retreat to return that love. More important, the *Spiritual Exercises* lead to a love which, in imitation of God in Christ, expresses itself in deeds more than in words.

The need both to be loved and to be able to love in return is elemental to human existence. But what the *Spiritual Exercises* represent is an experience which bases love on personal worth and responsibility and not on appetite. There is enduring worth in such an experience. Universities are not sensitivity sessions, but they are places where young men and women can come to comprehend their own worth as well as their responsibility for others. These students either cultivate the power to love as adults or they become trapped in self-doubt, self-rejection, or the selfish exploitation of others. The *Spiritual Exercises* are part of that tradition which takes seriously the power love has to give life to ideas and to values.

Finally, the *Spiritual Exercises* are a call to responsible service. Within the context of the retreat, a person's life is integrated in the choice to lead a life of sustained Christian labor. The process leading to this choice is important for modern Americans. For if we are to see ourselves as part of a cherished tradition and find ourselves capable of being loved and of loving in return, then we must also reestablish a social and moral ecology in our times.

The *Spiritual Exercises* remind us of the value of great texts to inspire action and not just to prompt contemplation. Great texts transcend their paper and their type to touch the human heart, to remind us that peace is a blessing, that justice is the basis of society, that communication is a bridge to new experiences and friendships, that redemption is our destiny. The university is part of the wider human community—urban, national, and international. The corporate vocation of the university in research and teaching is to unite public and private interests into a common harmony. The abuses of vested interests meet us all daily in our press and in our TV.

The *Exercises*, as text and as experience, stand in that educational tradition which argues that those on whom talent, opportunity, and grace have been bestowed have a responsibility to work for a society and a world both more faithful and more just, for true social ecology.

CONCLUSION

The *Spiritual Exercises* are not Scripture. They have, however, helped me to pray Scripture with a sense of personal responsibility. The *Exercises* have led me back to God's Word and to the conviction that the heart of my vocation as a Jesuit and as an administrator is to know God and that the best knowledge of God is in the humanity of Jesus. I do not impose my vocation on others, but I would be unfaithful to its significance for me if I did not spell out its strength as one important way to lead human life.

Part of our agreed upon mission in this symposium was to give testimony of one's own search for excellence. Excellence in sustained religious identity, ministry, and leadership is how I personally would translate that. In many ways, I feel I am repeating what every Jesuit here who is over forty will recognize immediately, and the younger among us will wonder where it came from. There is a fine saying we used to hear once a month—that the manner of Jesuits is ordinary. What I am about to say describes a very ordinary Jesuit life. I think there are three phases of identity, ministry, and leadership which mark the development of men and women who seek to dedicate their lives to the love and service of God and other people.

First identity. I would see my own life somewhat in literary terms—that old *inclusio* which you might be familiar with: a statement of a proposition, the narration of the realities, and the conclusion in a restatement of that proposition, but now with new understanding and new depth from having gone through the experience. You find it frequently in Scripture. Jesus grew in wisdom and strength before man and God. You have the narration and then you have the kind of repetition of that formula at the end of that particular pericope. At the beginning of my own Jesuit life, we started with a thirty-day retreat in the sleepy suburbs of Cincinnati. It was a preached retreat. We gathered together five times a day and someone told us what we should pray about and how we should feel about what we prayed. Despite what I now feel was the absurdity of that structure, it worked. It gave us a group identity, it gave us values, it formed a kind of basis for fifteen years of living that out in Jesuit formation. At the end of those fifteen years, this time in North Wales, under a man who is a great exponent of the *Spiritual Exercises*, Paul Kennedy, I completed that part of my Jesuit life that gave me identity. I made what we call our final year—tertianship. This time I made the thirty-day retreat seeing my spiritual director only once every three days, hearing him, at most, maybe for ten minutes. It was an extremely isolating and yet tremendously solidifying experience for me of what the Exercises are about. I began and I ended my formation with that experience, and as I left tertianship, it struck me that there are three things that are important in any religious experience, in any religious text that invites not simply criticism, but loyalty, love, and adhesion. You have to repeat the experience. Anything that's worthwhile, anything in which we invest some religious caring, we have to go over again, and again, and again.

I'll use one example: Whenever I do feel down, one of my favorite texts is *Pride and Prejudice*. I've read it now something like twenty-five times. I like it because it reminds me of my mother, it reminds me of a woman I think I would like to have married and I didn't, partially because I think she could have done better. It reminds me also, in that repetition of what friendship is, that we know we don't become friends by instant intimacy. That's dangerous territory. We become friends by repeating and seeing one another in many kinds of circumstances, in pain and anguish, in joy and hilarity, in being together when we argue, and being together when we can be reconciled. There's nothing in a text or any investment in human relationship that doesn't deepen because we are willing to live with it and to let it repeat itself over us and within us.

Second, that repetition leads to an understanding, an understanding not of what I feel I should say about a text, but of what about it resonates within me as true and accurate, vital and part of my own life. And I really felt that about the Exercises. And finally, there was the best thing of all in that first stage of identity—a cherishment—that I could no more relinquish the reality of this religious text than I could my flesh or my blood or my own history. It has become part of the way in which I symbolize myself—as a man who has committed himself to a religious vocation, as a professional and as one in ministry. This identity is the real meaning of solitude that I mentioned before—the profound sense that it doesn't make much difference whether it's true for anyone else, it's a text that has meaning for me, and it invites me to ask others to find their meaning and to find whatever their transcendent treasure might be and not to lose it.

Third, this experience of the Exercises has lead me to an understanding of ministry. As a young priest, I gave my first retreat to something like four hundred Notre Dame sisters in Cleveland who were gathered together for their eight-day retreat. A horrendous experience, but somehow God writes straight with crooked lines. God also writes straight because you stayed up until one o'clock in those days, hearing confessions. At the end of that retreat, I went to say farewell to an elderly sister in the infirmary, who had been a great woman within her religious community. She was one of the first to get a doctorate; later on, she was president of one of their universities and a great builder, a tremendous woman. And now she was dying of multiple sclerosis. When I went to see her she said, "I made the Exercises with you through the pipeline that comes into the infirmary as they transcribed you from the chapel. And I want to say one thing to you because we shall never meet again on this earth. Remember what the Exercises are really about is what has happened to me. Years ago I thought what God wanted was my head and I studied as my own order wished me to and I got my doctorate. And then He called me from a promising career in research to take the burden of administration and to become president and to become a builder and I did. Then I thought, no, God didn't want my head, God wanted my hands, my labor, my efficiency. And now I can't remember names from one day to the next. I have lost my head. I can't even pick up that glass of water on the stand next to my table. God didn't want my hands. The only thing I can give, and I wish I'd given it so much sooner, is my heart. I want you to remember, as a young priest, that the center of what you are doing is in the heart. And what's far more important is the way in which human beings who feel that God has called them never lose their humanity or their thirst for God, but that they are a mystery because their hearts are so pure with love."

It's hard to forget people like that. That for me was almost twenty years ago, and it was a profound experience, and one that has stayed in my own sense of ministry and of what the Exercises are—a tenderness and a kind of immediacy. That gave me a kind of negative norm that any religious text which dehumanized a person was not for me

Ignatian or Christian, and any text that divinized humanity without any relation to God, was not human and was not Ignatian.

Later, as I moved through Jesuit formation as a man in charge of it, while teaching the Exercises at the Weston School of Theology to students from Harvard Divinity and from Boston University Divinity School, with their questions and with their arguing and their desires to fix on strategies rather than the heart, I found out what could happen to hard-nosed research students if I told them they could take an hour a day and just think in their own way about the kind of man or woman they wanted to be. If they wanted to take my course, I wanted them to pass the exam, I wanted them to know all the information and theory I would give them, but I also wanted them to take an hour a day to experience their soul. I am always happy about what happened with those experiences, because they taught me what it was to be generative, to give life to other people. Now, as a Jesuit provincial, as someone who is involved with a lot of in-church and in-house materials, someone who is not really in the public arena or academe anymore—I always say a doctorate for me was a doctorate for frustration—I look at what is happening in our own church and I think it is exciting and I think it is tremendously risky. We are at an age in which the free civil servants that the church had depended on for so long—priests and nuns and brothers—are not there. I do not know of any religious superior that I have talked to throughout the United States who does not realize that we simply do not have the resources we once had to carry out our vision or our strategies by ourselves. I think, unlike others, that this is a time of tremendous growth for the Christian community because the responsibility for being dedicated people is no longer the responsibility of some self-designated elite; it is the responsibility of a whole church. The challenge to surrender, in the spirit of the Exercises, and hand over all that has been done so that God can do it in God's way through God's people, is one I hope we will meet. I think it will be tremendously painful and risky, but it is a wonderful venture for us, and nowhere more venturesome than in higher education. When I look at the network of Jesuit universities, the demands for excellence, and the diminishment of our numbers, we have to cope with this, and we either do it according to expediencies or we take our religious text and make it real and vital for us by our willingness to surrender to the meaning of the kingdom.

Frederick Buechner, reflecting on the role of religion today, has offered a challenging commentary:

Certainly a Christian must speak to the world in the language of the world. He must make the noblest causes of the world his causes and fight for justice and peace with the world's weapons—with Xerox machines and demonstrations and social action. He must reach out in something like love to what he can see of Christ in every man. But I think he must also be willing to be fantastic, or fantastic in other ways too, because at its heart religious faith is fantastic.[8]

I believe Buechner. It is contemporary and relevant to struggle—for money, for prestige, for survival. The *Exercises*, like all great texts, offer an alternative. The *Exercises* say that it should be contemporary and relevant to struggle to love, to make love a vision and a strategy. Ultimately, I find the *Exercises* tell people like me that religion must end where it began—in God's love and in human response.

NOTES

1. On the genesis of the Spiritual Exercises, see Joseph de Guibert, S.J., *The Jesuits, Their Spiritual Doctrine and Practice* (Saint Louis: Institute of Jesuit Sources, 1972), 113-22.
2. *The Constitutions of the Society of Jesus* (Saint Louis: Institute of Jesuit Sources, 1970), note D, 357.
3. The best English commentary on this Contemplation is Michael J. Buckley, S.J., "The Contemplation to Attain Love," *The Way Supplement*, 24 (1975), 92-104.
4. This passage and all other citations of the *Exercises* are taken from the 1980 dual text edition of *The Spiritual Exercises of St. Ignatius: A Literal Translation and a Contemporary Reading* (St. Louis: Institute of Jesuit Sources). Elder Mullan, S.J. translated the sixteenth-century *Autograph* in 1909 and David L. Fleming, S.J. wrote the parallel interpretation in 1977.
5. Buckley, "Contemplation," 92-93.
6. E.g., Paul Begheyn, S.J., "A Bibliography on St. Ignatius' Spiritual Exercises: A Working-Tool for American Students," in *Studies in the Spirituality of Jesuits*, 13 (March 1981).
7. Michael J. Buckley, S.J., "Freedom, Election, and Self-Transcendence: Some Reflections upon the Ignatian Development of a Life of Ministry," in *Ignatian Spirituality in a Secular Age*, ed. George D. Schner (Waterloo, Ontario: Canadian Corporation for Studies in Religion, 1984), 65-90.
8. Frederick Buechner, *The Hungering Dark* (New York: Seabury Press, 1981), 122-23.

MICHAEL J. COLLINS

ON

Shakespeare's King Lear

Like many of Shakespeare's plays, *King Lear* seems, at first, the stuff of fairy tales. Once upon a time, there was a king who had three beautiful daughters. Since the king was very old and had ruled for many years, he decided to divide his kingdom among his three daughters. On the appointed day, he called together all the lords of his kingdom and commanded his daughters to declare, before all the assembly, which of them loved him most. First Goneril, the eldest daughter, spoke:

> Sir, I love you more than word can wield the matter;
> Dearer than eyesight, space and liberty;
> Beyond what can be valued, rich or rare;
> No less than life, with grace, health, beauty, honor;
> As much as child e'er loved, or father found;
> A love that makes breath poor, and speech unable:
> Beyond all manner of so much I love you.[1]

Even if you have never heard of the play before, you know what is going to happen. The two older sisters make elaborate, but obviously false, professions of love for their father and receive substantial slices of the kingdom in return. The youngest daughter, who in these stories is always virtuous, speaks simply and honestly, and her father, of course, disowns her. (While we may not, on reflection, endorse her response entirely, Shakespeare underlines Cordelia's honesty and draws our sympathy to her through the two asides—1.1.64 and 78-80—she addresses to the audience. "What shall Cordelia speak?" she asks in the first. "Love, and be silent.") Even the wise protestations of the king's faithful servant cannot save her, and he is finally banished for alone having the courage to tell the king what we and apparently the entire assembly know: he has been deceived by the guile and flattery of two wicked daughters.

You know what, in the fairy tale, happens next. Once they have their shares of the kingdom, the ungrateful older daughters treat their father cruelly, but he is ultimately saved by his younger daughter, her virtuous husband, and the banished servant. The wicked sisters are soon or late defeated, and in the end, father, daughter, husband, and faithful servant live happily ever after in the kingdom. When we have finished with the story and at last put out the lights, our children can sleep peacefully in their beds.

But *King Lear*, as you know, does not end that way. If Shakespeare wanted to write a fairy tale, he forgot to see justice get done and the people he brings us to care about live happily ever after. *King Lear* is more terrifying than comforting, and once we have seen it or read it, we may not sleep as peacefully as once we did. In *King Lear*, Shakespeare looks more deeply and directly than he does in any of his other plays at what the American poet Karl Shapiro calls "our richest horror,"[2] at the darkest possibility of the human condition. In *King Lear* nothing is given, not the smallest patch of ground on which to stand. We reel at the very edge of the abyss, look squarely into its horrifying depth, and whatever answers we make, whatever words we speak against chaos and darkness, must be earned in the play of people and events, in the existential complication of a fallen world. *King Lear* is a play for our time. In it Shakespeare tests all our shelters against the wild night and finally finds some small hovel in which men and women may risk an act of faith.

In *As You Like It*, the melancholy Jacques, in a characteristically cynical speech, enumerates what he calls the "seven ages" of every human life.

> All the world's a stage,
> And all the men and women merely players;
> They have their exits and their entrances,
> And one man in his time plays many parts,
> His acts being seven stages. At first, the infant,
> Mewling and puking in the nurse's arms.
> Then the whining schoolboy, with his satchel
> And shining morning face, creeping like a snail
> Unwillingly to school. And then the lover,
> Sighing like a furnace, with a woeful ballad
> Made to his mistress' eyebrow. Then a soldier,
> Full of strange oaths and bearded like the pard,
> Jealous in honor, sudden and quick in quarrel,
> Seeking the bubble reputation

Even in the cannon's mouth. And then the justice,
In fair round belly with good capon lined,
With eyes severe and beard of formal cut,
Full of wise saws and modern instances;
And so he plays his part. The sixth age shifts
Into the lean and slippered pantaloon,
With spectacles on nose and pouch on side;
His youthful hose, well saved, a world too wide
For his shrunk shank, and his big manly voice,
Turning again toward childish treble, pipes
And whistles in his sound. Last scene of all,
That ends this strange eventful history,
Is second childishness and mere oblivion,
Sans teeth, sans eyes, sans taste, sans everything.[3]

While the speech is at once qualified in the play by the generous welcome of the old servant Adam to the Duke's banquet table in itself it leaves no room for joy or optimism. *King Lear*, in a more terrifying and painfully particular way, focuses on the sixth and seventh age and traces the horrifying transformation that threatens us all: the reduction of a once able and autonomous human being to vacuity and dependence.

On the very day Goneril and Regan receive their shares of the kingdom, they cease their protestations of love and sound the all too familiar words of daughters everywhere who have aging, erratic fathers to deal with. Later, in act 1, scene 4, when Lear returns with his knights from hunting to Goneril's hall, the process of his disintegration begins. Goneril's servant first ignores him and then, when asked "Who am I, sir?" replies "My lady's father" (1.4.82). Goneril, in a speech whose diction and syntax suggest has been carefully rehearsed, chides him as though he were a child. As he senses eroding the roles which defined and gave him meaning, kingship and fatherhood, he cries out to his followers in ironic amazement:

Does any here know me? This is not Lear.
Does Lear walk thus? Speak thus? Where are his eyes?
Either his notion weakens, or his discernings
Are lethargied—Ha! Waking? 'Tis not so.
Who is it that can tell me who I am?

(1.4.232-36)

The fool's answer (1.4.237) is as insightful as it is brief: "Lear's shadow," he says. In another sixty lines, Lear's train of a hundred knights is cut in half.

Without sleep or supper, Lear rides throughout the night, first to Regan's and then to Gloucester's castle, where he finds that his servant has been stocked and his daughter and her husband refuse to speak with him. He moves between anger and anguish, between king and father, but now he is neither. "The King would speak with Cornwall. The dear father/Would with his daughter speak" (2.4.99-100). Goneril soon arrives, and together the two daughters, with the old man standing between on the stage, piece by piece reduce Lear's train to nothing and so leave him helpless and dependent without title or function.

> Goneril. Why might not you, my lord, receive attendance
> From those that she calls servants, or from mine?
> (2.4.242-43)

> Regan. Why not, my lord? If then they chanced to slack ye,
> We could control them. If you will come to me
> (For now I spy a danger), I entreat you
> To bring five-and-twenty. To no more
> Will I give place or notice.
> (2.4.244-48)

> Goneril. Hear me, my lord.
> What need you five-and-twenty? ten? or five?
> To follow in a house where twice so many
> Have a command to tend you?
> (2.4.259-62)

> Regan. What need one?
> (2.4.263)

Lear's response, "O reason not the need" (2.4.263), more plaintive than angry, is, no matter what its tone, an appeal for love. Whether or not he recognizes it, Lear asks his daughters to do what he could not: to ignore the arithmetic conclusions of so much land for so much love and so many knights for so many services and to give without calculation, out of love. Later in the play, touched by her own experience of Lear's suffering, Cordelia rejects her own naively arithmetic view of love in the opening scene—"Haply, when I shall wed,/That lord whose hand must take my plight shall carry/Half of my love with him" (102-4)—and when Lear tells her she has cause not to love him, she replies, with her characteristic reticence and simplicity, "No cause, no cause" (4.7.75). Cordelia is the one daughter in whom compassion and generosity override logic and calculation. Her simple response, "No cause, no cause," is, in its context, a resonant and moving declaration of her love.

No matter what we make of Lear's initial decision to divide his kingdom and retain a hundred knights, in the scene with Goneril and Regan we witness, in a few intense and troubling moments on the stage, not simply the terrible process of aging which the melancholy Jacques describes in *As You Like It* ("sans teeth, sans eyes, sans taste, sans everything"), but also the perverse triumph of sensible efficiency over slovenly compassion. As I sit in my office, trying to manage— successfully and effectively—my small corner of the university, I recognize the practical wisdom of Regan's question to Lear: "How in one house/Would many people under two commands,/Hold amity" (2.4.239-41)? A kingdom cannot have two kings, Willy Loman cannot represent the firm in Boston, some old people cannot live alone, the university cannot serve its students well with lazy, incompetent, tired, or indifferent people. But as those sensible, practical, efficient daughters reduce their aging, difficult father to vacuity and dependence, they make clear that such judgments on our fellows need be considered and compassionate. "Give him his knights," I say every time I see the play. "He has nothing else: he 'gave you all'"(2.4.249). "Give him his knights," I tell my students. "It's the way we have to live." As we watch the play, moved by Lear's painful disintegration, we come to understand that arithmetic answers are compelling only on paper, that in the world of our daily lives, as we strive to reconcile order and efficiency with generosity and compassion, cause should sometimes have no effect and one plus two should sometimes make a hundred.

With what often seems his last remaining strength, Lear, hungry and exhausted, struggles to resist the calculations of his daughters and, with a storm about to begin, goes out of Gloucester's castle to the heath. Although Gloucester intercedes for him, neither Goneril, Regan, nor her husband, the Duke of Cornwall, takes pity on him. "O, sir, to willful men/The injuries that they themselves procure/Must be their schoolmasters" (2.4.301-3). The words of Regan to Gloucester, "Shut up your doors" (303), are repeated three lines later by Cornwall, and as we hear the thud of doors closing on the stage, they become the refrain that underscores the terrible isolation and cruel neglect of "a man/More sinned against than sinning" (3.2.59-60). As Cornwall says again, "Shut up your doors, my lord; 'tis a wild night/My Regan counsels well," we begin to recognize, as the play will soon suggest, that the kingdom has been thrown into chaos and Lear brought to suffering not simply by the ingratitude of his children, but by the cruelty and indifference of a government.

Out on the heath, in the brawling storm of Act III, with his Fool and Kent, Lear suffers and grows compassionate. "Come on, my boy," he says to the Fool. "How dost, my boy? Art cold?/I am cold myself" (3.2.68-69). As he kneels to pray outside the hovel, he recognizes the failure of his kingship to care for those who suffer on the edges of the settled world.

> Poor naked wretches, wheresoe'er you are,
> That bide the pelting of this pitiless storm,
> How shall your houseless heads and unfed sides,
> Your looped and windowed raggedness, defend you
> From seasons such as these? O, I have ta'en
> Too little care of this! Take physic, pomp;
> Expose thyself to feel what wretches feel,
> That thou mayst shake the superflux to them,
> And show the heavens more just.
>
> (3.4.28-36)

If Lear learns the need for compassion in the storm, so too do we who witness it. Once we see Lear's suffering and feel compassion for him, we cannot simply close the book or leave the theatre and ignore what we have come to know in all its horror. As we watch this "poor, infirm, weak, and despised old man" (3.2.20), we are joined to all the aged, the homeless, the hungry, the destitute, the impoverished who, like him, seek shelter not just from wind and cold, but from the cruelty and indifference of individuals and institutions. Shut out with Lear from the shelter of the castle, suffering with him from the cruelty of his children and the self-interest of a government, we discover once again that, in both the public and private order, we "have promises to keep" to one another.[4]

Inside the castle, another, even more remarkable transformation takes place. Gloucester cannot put the suffering King Lear from his mind. For most of the play, Gloucester has been a great disappointment: bumbling, gullible, insensitive, ineffectual, he has been duped by his bastard son Edmund, flattered and made serviceable by Regan and Cornwall. In the first scene he recalls, in the presence of his son, "the good sport at his making" (1.1.23-4) (the last thing anyone wants to hear about is "the good sport at his making"), and he minimizes the evil that surrounds him by ascribing it to the "late eclipses in the sun and moon" (1.2.112). But he cannot forget the king. Although motivated in part by policy—"These injuries the king now bears will be revenged home" (3.3.12-13)—he cannot escape or avoid the decision that the evil of the world has forced upon him. With one of the most resonant and moving lines in the play, bumbling old Gloucester makes his courageous, superbly understated, existential recognition: "If I die for it, as no less is threatened me, the king my old master must be relieved" (3.3.18-19). He cites no principles, he makes no large claims, he offers no heroic statements. The plight of the king has made necessary and inescapable an act one imagines he would prefer to avoid. And so this very ordinary, all too human, rather silly old man, foolishly warning the son who will betray him to "be careful" (3.3.20-21), sets out in the storm to relieve the king.

As Gloucester's simple words suggest, we, as a society, as individuals, can never put a final end to suffering, never save the world. What we can do, if we are brave enough, if we are lucky, is to save men and women, one at a time, as their need becomes known to us in our daily round, as it makes compassion inescapable and draws from very ordinary people, whether they would or not, a generous or, at times, even a heroic response: "The king my old master must be relieved." Gloucester's words can temper the discouragement, the frustration, the despair we all feel at the overwhelming magnitude of suffering in our world, for, like the play in which they are spoken, they recognize that compassion and relief must take "a local habitation and a name."[5] Gloucester's heroic kindness to the king, which has significance as both a private and a public act, becomes, in the howl of cruelty and suffering, a whispered celebration of goodness in our world. As he arrives on the heath in the next scene with a torch in his hand, a point of light in a dark place, he qualifies Lear's despairing words that "unaccommodated man is no more but . . . a poor, bare, forked animal" (3.4.109-10). In the context of the play, the implication of Gloucester's decision is inescapable: as individuals, as a society, we must bring all our Lears "where . . . fire and food is ready" (3.4.156).

The Anglo-Welsh poet Glyn Jones, in "The Common Path," suggests the force of Gloucester's words.

> On one side the hedge, on the other the brook:
>   Each afternoon I passed, unnoticed,
> The middle-aged schoolmistress, grey-haired,
>   Gay, loving, who went home along the path.
>
> That spring she walked briskly, carrying her bag
>   With the long ledger, the ruler, the catkin twigs,
> Two excited little girls from her class
>   Chattering around their smiling teacher.

Summer returned, each day then she approached slowly,
>   Alone, wholly absorbed, as though in defeat
Between water and hazels, her eyes heedless,
>   Her grey face deeply cast down. Could it be
Grief at the great universal agony had begun
>   To feed upon her heart—war, imbecility,
Old age, starving, children's deaths, deformities?
>   I, free, white, gentile, born neither
Dwarf nor idiot, passed her by, drawing in
>   The skirts of my satisfaction, on the other side.

One day, at the last instant of our passing,
>   She became, suddenly, aware of me
And, as her withdrawn glance met my eyes,
>   Her whole face kindled into life, I heard
From large brown eyes a blare of terror, anguished
>   Supplication, her cry of doom, death, despair.
And in the warmth of that path's sunshine
>   And of my small and manageable success
I felt at once repelled, affronted by her suffering,
>   The naked shamelessness of that wild despair.

Troubled, I avoided the common until I heard
>   Soon, very soon, the schoolmistress, not from
Any agony of remote and universal suffering
>   Or unendurable grief for others, but
Private, middle-aged, rectal cancer, was dead.

What I remember, and in twenty years have
>   Never expiated, is that my impatience,
That one glance of my intolerance,
>   Rejected her, and so rejected all
The sufferings of wars, imprisonments,
>   Deformities, starvation, idiocy, old age—
Because fortune, sunlight, meaningless success,
>   Comforted an instant what must not be comforted.[6]

As I try to help my students and colleagues through difficult moments in their lives, to teach well both in and out of the classroom, I often wonder whether the work has any value, whether it makes any difference, particularly when the needs of others in Washington and the world beyond seem often so much greater than theirs. In those dark moments, I sometimes think of Gloucester and console myself by remembering that whatever good we do, we do, as he does, on the common path, for individual men and women, in the existential choices we make or, perhaps, cannot avoid making, in the daily events of our lives.

Although Kent prays that the gods will reward his kindness, the gods, if they exist at all, remain aloof: In one of Shakespeare's most horrifying scenes, Gloucester's eyes are plucked out for helping the king, and he is left by Cornwall and Regan to "smell/His way to Dover" (3.7.94-95). Kindness, compassion, courage are never rewarded in *King Lear*: Kent is banished, Gloucester is betrayed by his son and blinded, the servant who tries to save him is killed, Cordelia's army is defeated at Dover, and she is hanged in prison as her father futilely struggles to save her. The world of *King Lear* is frighteningly like our own, where the good are as likely to be destroyed as to triumph, where no god, to use the words of Gerard Manley Hopkins, making "shipwreck . . . a harvest," will be "fetched in the storm of his strides."[7] Neither Gloucester nor we who watch him, probably not as individuals, certainly not as a society, can ground a decision to relieve the king on the blessing of the gods.

King Lear suggests, perhaps more starkly than do any of Shakespeare's other plays, the evil of which this world is capable: it is banal, it is gratuitous, but it is evil nonetheless. The good are often destroyed by it, and the play refuses explicitly to affirm that the gods will see justice done, either in this world or in another. But as we witness in *King Lear* the possibilities for evil in the world, we come to recognize that although all three are dead at the end, "it is better," as the critic Maynard Mack puts it, "to have been Cordelia than to have been her sisters."[8] If we have only this existential world to live in, we want it to be Cordelia's world, not Goneril and Regan's, we want it shaped by justice and compassion, not by lust, greed, cruelty, and indifference.

And, as the play itself suggests, we have to choose. When, at the end of the battle at Dover, Lear and Cordelia are taken prisoner, the old man welcomes the opportunity to withdraw from the affairs of the world and to live privately, to be simply a good father to Cordelia.

> Come, let's away to prison:
> We two alone will sing like birds i' th' cage:
> When thou dost ask me blessing, I'll kneel down
> And ask of thee forgiveness: so we'll live,
> And pray, and sing, and tell old tales, and laugh
> At gilded butterflies, and hear poor rogues

> Talk of court news; and we'll talk with them too,
> Who loses and who wins, who's in who's out;
> And take upon's the mystery of things,
> As if we were God's spies: and we'll wear out,
> In a walled prison, packs and sects of great ones
> That ebb and flow by th' moon.
>
> (5.3.8-19)

It is a beautiful vision—a loving father and his daughter, free of the evil, the cruelty, the corruption of the world, Prospero and Miranda on their island. "Upon such sacrifices," Lear assures her, "the gods themselves throw incense" (5.3.20-21). But while the gods, as always, make no sign, Edmund motions to a captain and, as Lear and Cordelia are led away to prison, he hands him a commission to hang them both. We cannot, the play suggests, evade commitment.

Whenever I enter the world of *King Lear*, I am reminded of the poem W. H. Auden named for the date of Hitler's invasion of Poland, "September 1, 1939."[9]

> I sit in one of the dives
> On Fifty-second Street
> Uncertain and afraid
> As the clever hopes expire
> Of a low dishonest decade:
> Waves of anger and fear
> Circulate over the bright
> And darkened lands of the earth,
> Obsessing our private lives;
> The unmentionable odour of death
> Offends the September night.

Europe at the beginning of the war seems, as Auden describes it, the kingdom of Goneril and Regan:

> Defenceless under the night
> Our world in stupor lies;
> Yet, dotted everywhere,
> Ironic points of light
> Flash out wherever the Just
> Exchange their messages:
> May I, composed like them
> Of Eros and of dust,
> Beleaguered by the same
> Negation and despair,
> Show an affirming flame.

"Ironic points of light/Flash out" in *King Lear* as well, in the brave and compassionate acts of those who, like Cordelia, Kent, Gloucester, the servant of Cornwall, in their particular, existential choices on the common path, would move the kingdom toward all we know it should be. The world we live in is, in its way, as dark and terrifying as *King Lear*'s and Auden's in "September 1, 1939." We are given no comforting certitudes. Violence, indifference, cruelty, injustice assault us daily; the survival of our fragile earth is threatened by a single nuclear crash and the unremitting abuse of its riches. But in *King Lear*, I'd say, we find the ground upon which to act. In its vision of a world we know we must not have, we recognize the need to be Cordelia, the need "to show," in whatever ways are given us, "an affirming flame." Coincidentally, a revision Auden made to one of the lines in "September 1, 1939" suggests the kind of affirmation *King Lear* makes: it is not, as Auden originally wrote, "we must love one another or die," but rather, as he put it later, a tougher, more disturbing one: "we must love one another and die."[10] By suggesting, in painful and moving particularity, the cruelty, the injustice, the evil of which the world is capable, the play affirms, no matter what the human condition or its "promised end" (5.3.265), that "it is better to have been Cordelia."

Toward the end of act 3 scene 6, Gloucester returns to warn Kent of "a plot of death upon" Lear (88), and together they get him safely on his way to Dover where Cordelia's army is waiting. The play, at this point, puts its characters on the road: first Lear and Kent, then Gloucester and Edgar, and finally Goneril, Regan, and Edmund set out for what we know will be the climactic battle at Dover. As Kent recognizes at the end of act 4 (7.97-98), the battle will decide the fate of the kingdom and of the individuals in it. Like the great biblical journey of Jesus and His followers to Jerusalem, the journey to Dover will, for good or for ill, bring the story to its close.

The last act of the play, however, frustrates both our expectations and our desires. Lear and Cordelia are defeated and, as the critic Stephen Booth points out, even after Albany has taken command and Edmund has been wounded by his brother, the play does not make the expected conventional progress to its end.[11] Suddenly, a play that seems about to close is blown open again by the entry of a howling Lear with the dead Cordelia in his arms. Kent's question, "Is this the promised end" by which he means the day of doom, is, in a different sense, ours as well. Is this the end the play has promised? Does Lear's painful coming to knowledge and compassion earn him nothing? Can we not say, at least at the very end, that the world is good, that things do somehow make sense, that God is in His heaven? Can no centurion find the words by which chaos is kept at bay and evil finally defeated? Can no one affirm, as Hopkins does of the five nuns in "The Wreck of the *Deutschland*," that Cordelia will "bathe in his fall-gold mercies" and "breathe in his all fire-glances" (vol. 1.57)? Is Lear's howl the only possible response?

The play remains throughout true to the existential complexity of the fallen world it so rigorously reflects and never once, even at its end, offers the comfort of an easy answer. Albany moves to end the play with a conventional affirmation that order and justice have been at last restored to the kingdom.

> You lords and noble friends, know our intent.
> What comfort to this great decay may come
> Shall be applied. For us, we will resign,
> During the life of this old majesty,
> To him our absolute power: you, to your rights;
> With boot, and such addition as your honors
> Have more than merited. All friends shall taste
> The wages of their virtue, and all foes
> The cup of their deservings.
>
> (5.3.298-306)

But the play does not end here. Lear makes some movement on the stage which interrupts Albany's speech and then begins his last lament over the body of Cordelia.

> And my poor fool is hanged: no, no, no life?
> Why should a dog, a horse, a rat, have life,
> And thou no breath at all? Thou'lt come no more,
> Never, never, never, never, never.
>
> (5.3.307-10)

He pauses and, in a poignant and beautiful act of love, asks some bystander—Kent perhaps—to undo a button at the neck of his strangled daughter. And then he speaks his final words: "Do you see this? Look on her. Look, her lips,/Look there, look there" (312-13).

What does Lear see in that last moment of his life? What is the tone of those last words? The play is too honest, too true to the conditions by which we must live our lives ever to answer such questions. Some say Lear sees Cordelia living once again, others that he sees only an obscene spectacle, the absurd insult of her dead body. But the play says nothing, and the actor is left to choose, without certainty, between anguish and joy (or some gradation between them), because *King Lear* brings us to the edge of "The undiscovered country, from whose bourn/No traveler returns,"[12] because it asks a question to which no one can, with certainty, reply: do we live finally in a sane or a lunatic universe?

In discussing *Waiting for Godot*, a play which has certain affinities with *King Lear*, Samuel Beckett said, "There is a wonderful sentence in Augustine . . . 'Do not despair: one of the thieves was saved. Do not presume: one of the thieves was damned.'"[13] As Lear kneels over the dead body of Cordelia, poised, as the critic Barbara Everett, quoting Pascal, describes it, between everything and nothing,[14] we must, like the play itself, neither despair nor presume. While *King Lear* takes us to the edge of the abyss and insists we look squarely into it, while it "spatters," to quote Karl Shapiro's "Auto Wreck" once again, "all we knew of denouement" (vol. 2.391), it will not finally give way to despair. Do not despair, it tells us: Lear may see Cordelia living. Do not presume, it tells us: Lear may see Cordelia dead.

I want to look, for a moment, at another great text. In the middle of Mark's Gospel, Jesus takes Peter, James, and John "up into a high mountain."[15] There, he is "transfigured before them," and "his raiment," Mark writes, "became shining, exceeding white as snow; so as no fuller on earth can white them." In an instant, the three disciples see answered unambiguously the question everyone in Galilee has been asking, "Who is this man?" But just as quickly, the vision is gone, and the disciples, with Jesus the teacher beside them, make their way back down the mountain to a finite, ambiguous, fallen world where, like the rest of us, they will have to find a way to live without the splendid vision of the mountain top. *King Lear* is rooted in that finite, ambiguous, fallen world: no gods speak from out of the clouds, and its only mountain vision is the bogus one Edgar fabricates for his blind father to heal his despair. In *King Lear*, it seems to me, Shakespeare risks all by which we make sense of our lives, raises the darkest possibility of the human condition—that we stand ultimately on the sliding sand of a lunatic universe—and still affirms that, since we live without certainty, we dare not despair.

Whenever I read *King Lear*, whenever I discuss it with my students, I try to meet as best I can the demands of the text, to face its rich complexity and ambiguity with honesty, tenacity, and courage, as I believe Shakespeare faced the complexity and ambiguity of the world when he wrote the play, as I would hope to face them in the days of my own life. If we are honest, we find no easy answers either in *King Lear* or in the world it reflects, but we must all give answers nonetheless. Like audiences at the end of *King Lear*, we inevitably live with doubt and ambiguity in the classroom, on the job, in society, and in the remotest corners of our hearts. Poised between everything and nothing, in the text and in the world, we can do no more than read with care and make what seem the right choices along the way. If we do it well, if we work at it, if we are honest, tenacious, and brave, then we may find out truth where it hides—between certitude and skepticism, between presumption and despair.

No matter how often I see the dying Lear kneeling over the dead Cordelia, no matter how often I read the script, I never know with certainty what, if anything, Lear sees, what he asks me to look at. And since I never shall know, I try to keep my balance, in the text and in the world, to resist both the arrogance of presumption and the indifference of despair, to whisper, as I think the play does, a halting act of faith in the ultimate sanity of the world, to affirm, now out of the very uncertainty the play engenders, since I cannot prove the opposite, that "it is better to have been Cordelia." But then, if we live at all, we inevitably place a bet, if only implicitly, through the choices that we make. And so, in the last scene, if I were the actor, I'd speak Lear's words with joy, for I'll wager, in the end, Cordelia lives.

NOTES

1. William Shakespeare, *The Tragedy of King Lear*, ed. Russell Fraser, Signet Classic Shakespeare (New York: New American Library, 1963), I.i.57-63. Subsequent citations appear in the text.
2. Karl Shapiro, "Auto Wreck," in *Chief Modern Poets of Britain and America*, eds. Gerald DeWitt Sanders, John Herbert Nelson, and M. L. Rosenthal (Toronto: Macmillan, 1970), vol. 2, 390.
3. William Shakespeare, *As You Like It*, ed. Albert Gilman, Signet Classic Shakespeare (New York: New American Library, 1963), II.vii.139-66.
4. Robert Frost, "Stopping By Woods on a Snowy Evening," in Sanders, Nelson, and Rosenthal, vol. 2, 82.
5. William Shakespeare, *A Midsummer Night's Dream*, ed. Wolfgang Clemen, Signet Classic Shakespeare (New York: New American Library, 1963), V.i.17.
6. Glyn Jones, "The Common Path," in *Anglo-Welsh Poetry 1480-1980*, eds. Raymond Garlick and Roland Mathias (Bridgend, Mid Glamorgan: Poetry Wales Press, 1984), 160.
7. Gerard Manley Hopkins, "The Wreck of the Deutschland," in Sanders, Nelson, and Rosenthal, vol. 1, 59.
8. Maynard Mack, *King Lear in Our Time* (Berkeley and Los Angeles: University of California Press, 1965); reprinted in *Twentieth Century Interpretations of "King Lear"*, ed. Janet Adelman (Englewood Cliffs, N.J.: Prentice-Hall, 1978), 69.
9. W. H. Auden, "September 1, 1939," in Sanders, Nelson, and Rosenthal, vol. 1, 366-68.

10. Quoted in John Fuller, *A Reader's Guide to W. H. Auden* (New York: Farrar, Straus and Giroux, 1970), 260.
11. Stephen Booth, "On the Greatness of *King Lear*," in *"King Lear," "Macbeth," Indefinition and Tragedy* (New Haven: Yale University Press, 1983), 26-27.
12. William Shakespeare, *The Tragedy of Hamlet, Prince of Denmark*, ed. Edward Hubler, Signet Classic Shakespeare (New York: New American Library, 1963), III.i.79-80.
13. Quoted in Martin Esslin, *The Theater of the Absurd*, 3d ed. (Harmondsworth, England: Penguin Books, 1980), 53.
14. Barbara Everett, "The New *King Lear*," *Critical Quarterly* 2 (Winter 1960); reprinted in *"King Lear": A Selection of Critical Essays*, ed. Frank Kermode (London: Macmillan, 1969), 200.
15. Mark 9:2-3, King James Version.

WILLIAM WINTER

ON

The Essays of Ralph Waldo Emerson

It was my good fortune to have grown up in a home remote, isolated by today's standards, ten miles by winding gravel road from the nearest town, without radio, without television, without electricity, that nevertheless had a bookcase filled with great books. Both my father and mother were avid readers. My mother taught me in a little one-room school in the first and second grades. My father introduced me to the pleasures of reading.

An ardent Jeffersonian, he had me reading a biography of his hero when I was eight years old. It was out of this early exploration at home, plus the encouragement of inspired teachers in my elementary school and in my high school years at Grenada, that I came to regard writers with the same affection that I lavished on other less literarily-inclined heros like "Dizzy" Dean and Carl Hubbell.

In those growing-up years, I favored real-life stories. History and biography took precedence over the English classics, although my father insisted on some of the latter. He had, for instance, acquired through inheritance from an aunt all of the Waverly novels, and he had read every single one of them. But as I recall, *Ivanhoe* was as far as I got.

My English teacher was a great lady from Durant named Estelle Turner. She assigned me summer reading each summer during my high school years, reading that included folks like Thackeray and Dickens. But for some indefinable reason, I was attracted to the writers of my own country. I identified with the stories of Irving and Hawthorne and James Fenimore Cooper. Longfellow was my poet, as he wrote of "The Big Sky Water" and the haunting bayous of my own South. But I also liked Sidney Lanier—and Grantland Rice and Walter Stewart, who wrote sports for *The Memphis Commercial Appeal*.

It was almost by accident that I discovered Ralph Waldo Emerson. Miss Turner was not happy with my recitation one day; I had been reading too much Walter Stewart and Grantland Rice. So if I was to return to her good graces, she informed, it would be only after I had read and reported on Emerson's *Self-Reliance*. So on a lovely fall weekend, more suited to hunting squirrels on my father's place than plodding through the dusty tomes of a long-deceased New England writer, I reluctantly found a new and challenging world.

In an era when young people were growing up in Mississippi not encouraged to embrace different ideas, I found Emerson encouraging me to be a non-conformist. At a time when one dared challenge the old shibboleths at his peril, I was reading that "nothing is at last sacred but the integrity of our own mind." When the admonition of my elders and the pressure of my peers combined to dictate what was acceptable, I was being told by this Yankee from Massachusetts that I must trust only myself. Nothing that I had read before had such a profound and direct effect on my thinking. It was the beginning of my education.

Emerson in a simpler time helped prepare me for the infinitely more complex world in which I would spend my life. His essays defined more clearly than anything else that I had ever read the process of sorting out the ideas that we live by, of deciding what to keep and what to throw away, of testing what is proven and what is false. It is through the establishment of this value system that we really find out who we are, and it is also the means that decides our relationship to everyone else.

Emerson seemed to be writing particularly for my generation of young southerners. Growing up as we did in the middle of the Great Depression when hope and optimism fired by Roosevelt's New Deal were then beginning to replace the stolid conformity of the past, he asked the right questions of us. Why were we so timid, and imitative, and compliant? Why did we look backward so much, back to the so-called "good old days"? Why did we automatically fear, and thus resist, change? Why did we cling to herd instinct that was based on nothing more noble than mere survival?

Self-Reliance was an affirmation of faith in America. It was an affirmation of a commitment to the here-and-now, and to the opportunity that the future held. It was not, however, an advocacy of the selfish and superficial trends that tended to mark America's later society. Emerson was writing primarily for the young idealists of his day, but he was really writing for the young at heart of every generation. He put in perspective the temptations of selfish gain in calling on his readers to eschew a vulgar, self-directed prosperity, in raising to a national cause freedom of thought and action. His essay was almost like the quiet admonition of the commander on the battlefield just before the charge. He stressed the difficulty of the task, but he underlined it with the glory of the achievement. There would be weariness, insult, misunderstanding, and failure, but the reward would be the exhilaration of living in a truly satisfying way.

He wrote of the tenacity that is required in sticking to the accomplishment of a worthy purpose. Life was not a voyage for the shortwinded or the faint-hearted, and there would be no easy victories, at least no meaningful easy victories. Even the ones we did win would insure no permanent happiness. External achievement did not guarantee internal contentment. Emerson wrote about that as follows:

"A political victory, a rise of rents, the recovery of your sick, or the return of your absent friend, or some other quiet external event raises your spirits, and you think good days are preparing for you. Do not believe it. It can never be so. Nothing can bring you peace but yourself. Nothing can bring you peace but the triumph of principles."

This essay has frequently been misinterpreted as relying on our human qualities to the exclusion of faith in God. I have not read it that way. Emerson simply rejects the perception of the voice of God as belonging to some other distant age.

At a time when I was being weighed down by a sense of Calvinistic guilt as a Presbyterian, I heard Emerson say this:

"The relations of the soul to divine spirit are so pure that it is profane to seek to interpose help. If, therefore, a man claims to know and speak of God, and carries you backward to the phraseology of some old molded nation in another country, in another world, believe him not. That man is timid and apologetic. He is no longer upright. He dares not say, 'I think. I am,' but quotes some saint or sage.

"He is ashamed before the blade of grass or the blowing rose. These roses under my window make no reference to former roses or to better ones. They are for what they are. They exist with God today."

It was not long after I read this that William Alexander Percy from Greenville, Mississippi wrote *Lanterns on the Levee*. His memorable last chapter in that book was for me a remarkable affirmation of Emerson's insistence on the dignity of man in the sight of God. The parallel is so striking that the final paragraph of *Lanterns on the Levee* suggests that Percy himself, although he disclaims it in his book, was influenced by Emerson, possibly during Percy's years at Harvard, in his views of religion and of God.

Emerson's insistence on aspiring to standards of performance, of morality, and of taste above the commonplace has special meaning, particularly in light of today's emphasis on the commercially driven establishment of what is popular and what is acceptable. In this era of television commercials, which subtly and, often, not so subtly suggest what we should wear, and eat, and drink, and put on our hair, and what will make us irresistible to the opposite sex, it is helpful to be reminded of Emerson's rejection of mediocrity and blind conformity. He calls for an elevation of private responsibility. His highest aspiration for the nation was the development of a broad-based citizen leadership that would by its own high standards of performance and example create a national commitment to excellence.

> "Why all this deference to kings?" he writes. "Suppose they were virtuous? Do they wear out virtue? As great a stake depends on your private act today as followed their public and renowned steps. When private men shall act with original views, the luster will be transferred from the actions of kings to those of gentlemen."

The *Essay on Heroism* follows in the same vein. It is an appeal to a quality of living that is based on "an obedience to a secret impulse of an individual's character." Like *Self-Reliance* it cries out to the idealism of young people to forego the easy standards and conventions of society and look to a more exciting and challenging course. Again, he cites the essential quality of persistence:

> "The characteristic of genuine heroism is its persistence. All men have wandering impulses, fits and starts of generosity. But when you have resolved to be great, abide by yourself and do not weakly try to reconcile yourself with the world. The heroic cannot be common, nor the common heroic. It was a high counsel that I once heard given to a young person, 'Always do what you are afraid to do.'"

One of the most novel, yet valuable pieces of advice that this essay contains addresses the problem confronted by all of us at times when we are obligated to weigh our choices. The most inhibiting aspect of many decisions revolves around the concern of how we shall be perceived if we fail. We guard jealously our dignity lest we appear foolish. Nonsense, responds Emerson. "Has nature covenanted with me," he writes, "that I should never appear to disadvantage, never make a ridiculous figure? Let us be generous of our dignity, as well as of our money."

Another example of the heroic figure which he cites is that of one who is not ostentatious in his heroism. He simply is oblivious to both the plaudits and the criticisms of others. His motives provide their own reward. Temperance is the mark of the hero. Although he does not come across as a fanatical and solemn reformer, Emerson commends the person who does not require the stimulus of tobacco, drugs, or strong drink. He quotes John Elliott, who said of wine, "It is a noble and generous liquor, and we should be humbly thankful for it. But as I remember, water was made before it was."

Finally, Emerson restates the prices of heroism. It is no easy street. There is no usual *quid pro quo*:

"The heroic soul does not sell its justice and its nobleness. It does not ask to dine nicely and to sleep warm. The essence of greatness is the perception that virtue is enough. Poverty is its ornament. Plenty does not need it and can very well abide its loss."

In his *Essay on Politics*, which has special meaning for some of us, Emerson, while expressing perhaps an overly naive and idealistic view of the subject, nevertheless provides an incisive analysis of the two political parties. And a century and a half later, this is basically accurate in describing the parties today. This is how he analyzed them in 1844:

"Of the two great parties which at this hour almost share the nation between, I should say that one has the best cause, and the other contains the best men. The philosopher, the poet, or the religious man will, of course, wish to cast his vote with the Democrat—for free trade, for wide suffrage, for the abolition of legal cruelties in the penal code, and for facilitating in every manner the access of the young and the poor to the sources of wealth and power. But he can rarely accept the persons whom the so-called popular party proposes to him as representatives of those liberalities.

"On the other side, the Conservative Party, composed of the most moderate, able, and cultivated part of the population is timid and merely defensive of property. It vindicates no right, it aspires to no real good, it brands no crime, it proposes no generous policy, does not build, nor write, nor cherish the arts, nor foster religion, nor establish schools, nor defend the poor or the Indian or the immigrant."

Then in a sentence that indicts both parties, Emerson expressed his sense of disillusionment with practical politics:

"From neither party when in power, has the world any benefit to expect in science, arts, or humanity at all commensurate with the resources of the nation."

He did not, however, despair for the country. He saw its salvation in the capacity of people to adapt out of their needs to an irregular kind of common judgment. And reaching this conclusion, he used the following comparison between a monarchy and a republic.

"A monarchy is a merchantman which sails well, but which will sometimes strike on a rock and go to the bottom. While a republic is a raft which will never sink, but then your feet are always in the water."

He deplored the politics of popular passion. An advocate of natural law, he held firmly to the notion that legislative abuses would be corrected in time by the logic of natural events. Emerson described the process this way:

"Our statute is a currency which we stamp with our own portrait. It soon becomes unrecognizable, and in process of time will return to the mint. As fast as the public mind is open to more intelligence, the code is seen to be brute and stammering. Meantime, the education of the general mind never stops."

Emerson argued against the folly of attempting to impose our form of government on other nations. He warned against the cult of personality in the selection of political leaders. In an era of repressive monarchies in Europe and Asia, he called for this country to set an example for the world by putting the advancement of learning and commerce ahead of arms and military force. A complete idealist, he suggested a totally revolutionary ideal in a world which in the century that would follow would see some of the most savage and deadly wars in history. His proposal, that "the power of love is the basis of a state," has never been tried. But he also understood why it had not:

"For according to the order of nature, which is quite superior to our will, it stands thus. There will always be a government of force where men are selfish."

Thomas Wolfe, another of my heroes, who like Will Percy spent some time at Cambridge, may have been influenced by those Emersonian words when he wrote these words in *You Can't Go Home Again*:

> "I think the true discovery of America is before us. I think the true fulfillment of our spirit is yet to come. I think the enemy is here before us, too. I think the enemy is here before us with a thousand faces, but I think we know that all his faces wear one mask. I think the enemy is simple selfishness and compulsive greed."

Wolfe and Emerson apparently were studying the same book. Emerson insisted that, if his proposal of a political system based on love and brotherhood could work, it would be the basis for achieving our national destiny:

> "When men are pure enough to abjure the code of force, they will be wise enough to see how these public ends of the post office, of the highway, of the commerce and the exchange of property, of museums and libraries, of institutions of art and science can be answered.

While distrustful of the political process and the politicians who pursued it, he recognized its noble and fundamental basis. "Governments have their origins," he wrote, "in the moral identity of people."

The genius of Emerson has been perpetuated in the thinking and writing of many others who have shared his thoughts and been inspired by his classic idealism. It is a distressing commentary on our own age that the forces that Emerson railed against, the unthinking public judgments, now made more pervasive by the influence of television, have rendered infinitely more difficult the maintenance of individually held values.

Still, he remains what he established himself to be in the mid-19th century—a man of rare and professional understanding of the delicate and sensitive nature of the individual's relationship to himself, as well as to all mankind.

To read his works is to have a deeper knowledge of ourselves as we pursue this miraculous and mystifying journey that we call life.

ATHOL FUGARD

ON

Henry David Thoreau's Walden

Browsing through my now well-thumbed copy of Thoreau's *Walden*, I came predictably to one of my favorite paragraphs, because I love it so much, the book always falls open just at that point. I suppose the paragraph has a certain relevance to this occasion (as you will see, the fact that you are there, and I am here, and there is a healthy space between the two of us makes it to a certain extent relevant), but to be absolutely frank, my reason for reading it is selfish. I love it, and I want to try it out on an audience.

In my paragraph Thoreau is talking about an aspect of his life in a little cabin he built himself beside Walden Pond:

> "One inconvenience I sometimes experienced in so small a house was the difficulty of getting to a sufficient distance from my guest when we began to utter the big thoughts in big words. You want room for your thoughts to get into sailing trim and run a course or two before they make their port. The bullet of your thought must have overcome its lateral and ricochet motion and fallen into its last and steady course before it reaches the ear of the hearer, else it may plow out again through the other side of his head. Also, our sentences wanted room to unfold and form their columns in the interval.

> "Individuals, like nations, must have suitable broad and natural boundaries, even a considerable ground, between them. I have found it a singular luxury to talk across the pond to a companion on the opposite side. In my house, we were so near that we could not begin to hear. We could not speak low enough to be heard as when you throw two stones into calm water so near that they break each other's undulations. If we are merely loquacious and

loud talkers, then we can afford to stand very near together, cheek by jowl, and feel each other's breath. But if we speak reservedly and thoughtfully, we want to be further apart that all animal heat and moisture may have a chance to evaporate."

Now, I hold out no promise of big thoughts in big words, but I will try to speak reservedly and thoughtfully to you this morning. I had the good fortune to read *Walden* at exactly the right moment in my life, and what made that moment right was because it was the moment when I needed it. These words came to me at a point when I was in need of a simple statement of faith. My good fortune was that I had the book open and at my bedside at that precise moment. I believe that there is a point in everybody's life when they need *Walden*.

As I visit Georgetown today, another autumn has arrived. To be precise, I think it did so at about 3:20 on Thursday afternoon last week. If I remember correctly, that is when the announcement was made. I don't know who determines these things, whether it's the weathermen or astronomers, but at 3:20 last Thursday autumn arrived. It's not as obvious here in Washington as I thought it would be. I come to you from a little town about 50 miles north of New York City, and up there the woods are already (what would be the correct way to describe it?) incandescent with the colors of this extraordinary event that comes your way as Americans every year.

In the weeks preceding this moment, I had wondered whether I would be as struck, as amazed by the fall here in America as I was the first time I saw it. I think, apart from pictures and film images, I really first saw an American fall, a New England fall, only about 5 or 6 years ago, and I couldn't help wondering when it started to happen this time, whether I would be as impressed as I was on that first occasion. I wondered whether the novelty might have worn off like a fireworks display that goes on for a few seconds too long and leaves you feeling a little jaded at the end.

But no, when those trees started turning along the road in New York where I live, I was as stunned as I was on that first occasion. And you must understand that for me as a South African the effect is doubly enhanced. There is nothing like it at all in the part of Africa that I come from. We have a cycle of seasons (and they are as specific as the cycle of seasons you live through), but the contrasts are in no way as dramatic and as powerful. Compared with summer in South Africa, for example, which is very often dry and in need of rain, your summer is a lunatic season. I've never seen such growth. I have a little American garden, and I have watched the first timid entry of spring. Spring is very, very, very nervous and very, very reluctant to arrive, and rightly so, because of the possibility of frost and late snows. But once it has made its timid entry and prepared the way for summer, everything then just grows and goes mad! There's nothing like it back home.

So although the cycle of South African seasons is as specific as yours, the contrasts here are infinitely more dramatic. Even so, the cycle of emotions which I live through, with which I respond to the passage of seasons in the course of a year are the same whether I am on African soil or on American soil. We all know what spring means. We all know how splendid a reality summer is. We all know about that long, still, cold waiting winter; and now it's autumn, and autumn gives me my edge into—my springboard into—the aspect of Thoreau that I want to talk to you about.

Now, just before I do that, another way of preparing for my statement is to tell you about an extraordinary, an illustrious countryman of mine, a fellow South African, an Afrikaner. His name was Eugene Maret, and he is, I think, best known in South Africa now as a wonderful poet, but as a poet in Afrikaans, he is possibly not known to the world as a poet. He is certainly known to the world as a famous naturalist. Maret was particularly fascinated by evolution. His particular interest was the evolution of human consciousness, and his subject in studying it was the baboon of Africa.

Through his studies of the baboon, he concluded that, in the course of a day, twilight, those few gray hours between the setting of the sun and the onset of darkness, was a time of singular vulnerability for the human psyche and posed a particular challenge to it. He noticed that at the particular moment in the day after the sun had set, a troop of baboons, having foraged for food and full of *joie de vivre*, would turn in the direction of the setting sun and, for the brief period that twilight lasted, adopt an attitude of profound dejection as it lived through that moment when light left the world and darkness set in. Maret coined the phrase "hysperian depression" to describe that absolutely unvarying pattern of behavior. Every day of their lives, at twilight, the baboons would sit on the rocks and watch the westering sun disappear. Some of them would almost take on a keening as it went. And he rightly concluded (because further research has gone on to substantiate the point) that for a mind in transition between a life completely dominated by instinct and a life dominated by conscious thought, that moment of twilight was a period of singular vulnerability.

Now I think there's a parallel: in terms of the evolution of the human psyche (or, we might say the "human spirit") in a broader context, autumn has presented the same sort of challenge to man. We know what winter is about. We know that we have to live through it, but with the certain faith that spring will return. And then, when spring does return, we know all about the extraordinary sense of renewal that it gives us. When we see the earth renew itself, we ourselves in a sense live through an experience of renewal. But autumn is a challenge to our faith in renewal, and in that challenge, it has been one of the major milestones in the evolution of the human spirit. It has helped us understand and focus on the mystery of renewal, and that sense of mystery, for all that science has done to explain what we see, that sense of miracle if you like, remains strong in us today. That mystery is central to most of the religions of the world, a foundation of religious faith.

Now, as human beings, we are ourselves capable of a very grand and spectacular form of renewal. Myself—I am at a loss to say whether I was lucky or, as I sometimes felt, unlucky—I had the opportunity to experience at the age of 50 a massive renewal of my life. In one of her journals, May Sarton, that wonderful American writer, asks the question, asks herself, "Is it possible for our life to be renewed at the age of 60, completely renewed, completely changed at the age of 60?" I don't know about 60, but I do know about 50, and I do know that renewal happened to me. So, the whole concept of renewal, the notion of it, is one that I have lived with very seriously for many years now, and it is one that is progressively informing my work as a writer, more and more. I was very tempted in coming to you today to spend my time, to use this opportunity, to relate Thoreau to that big event, to the big renewal in my own life. But I decided against it, because I think there is an experience of renewal at a much more prosaic and fundamental level which is possibly even more challenging simply because it is at a more prosaic and fundamental level. And that level is where I would like to share what thoughts I have about Thoreau and his meaning to me.

Now, the quote from Thoreau is a very short one, and it strikes right to the heart of what I want to share with you.

These are the few luminous sentences:

"I know of no more encouraging fact than the unquestionable ability of man to elevate his life by a conscious endeavor. It is something to be able to paint a particular picture, or to carve a statue, and so to make a few objects beautiful, but it is far more glorious to carve and paint the very atmosphere and medium through which we look which morally we can do. To affect the quality of the day, that is the highest art."

I would like to read it again:

"I know of no more encouraging fact than the unquestionable ability of man to elevate his life by a conscious endeavor. It is something to be able to paint a particular picture, or to carve a statue, and so to make a few objects beautiful, but it is far more glorious to carve and paint the very atmosphere and medium through which we look which morally we can do. To affect the quality of the day, that is the highest art."

Now, I don't know about you, but as terrified as I am up here, I cannot but help thrilling to those words. Thoreau calls his statement a fact. I think his vocabulary is too modest. I think that with those words he has framed one of the handful of spiritual truths that man has garnered during the brief span of time he has been on this earth. It is fundamental and perennial because it is a truth that needs to be rediscovered, re-realized, re-lived, restated, by every new generation. I don't doubt that there have been a hundred as eloquent and precise formulations of that truth about renewal, or the ability of an individual human being to renew his life. I don't doubt that there have been a hundred as eloquent and precise formulations of that truth since Thoreau first formulated his beside Walden Pond 170 years ago. My good luck, as I said earlier, was that I encountered his when I needed it.

Now, I remember the occasion very clearly. It was near midnight, and I was propped in a bed in a Johannesburg hotel room. I had the book at my bedside. It had become my bedtime reading for about a week or so. An American friend had given it to me amazed that I had not read *Walden*.

I remember the day particularly clearly because it had been truly awful. Apart from hard and seemingly fruitless labor in a rehearsal room on a new play, the day's headlines had been about unbelievable police brutality, further detentions, and amongst those detained were a few of my friends, close personal friends. My walk between the hotel where I was staying and the rehearsal room had been through a Johannesburg crowded with jobless, homeless, hungry black men and women. Moving around in the city that day had, in fact, felt like floundering in a bog, in a morass of human misery and suffering from which there was seemingly no possibility of ever reaching hard, firm ground. It sort of climaxed. That particular day, I remember, climaxed for me a progressive sense of defeat. I mean, I love my country and its people passionately, and I have tried to live a life and do work by way of what I am best equipped to do which is to make theater. I have tried to live a life which would make some contribution to the situation there, to help bridge a terrible chasm, a terrible gap between the reality of a racist dominated society and the ideal of a society where something resembling democracy prevailed. But instead of seeing that hope and that vision realized, the years have only seen it actually eroded away. The situation in South Africa has only got worse; it has not improved. And when I return to my country in 4 or 5 weeks' time I know that I will be returning to a South Africa that is even worse now than it was on that particular night.

But to get back to that particular night. My sense of defeat, and of being useless and of having lived a life that had little effect on society, was very painful.

Now, the paragraph I stumbled upon, the paragraph I read to you from Thoreau was, in fact, the hard ground that I needed under my feet and has remained so ever since. I think it drew my attention to the fact that there is an area in my life, in which I am nobody's victim other than my own. I think those lines are focused on and draw attention to the fact that as human beings we have something called a soul, and that the quality of that soul is something that we determine, and which nobody else can interfere with if you choose to keep it that way.

In the course of the 56 years that I have lived, through my student years, through my early manhood, I have tried to subscribe to many different theories about what living a life meant. I know that I passed through my phase of thinking I was a Socialist, possibly even a Communist, and that I saw man as something that was made and determined by social factors and social circumstances, and that they were of over-riding importance, and that a man could only be made a good man. A good man needed to have a good society. I have gone through all the various variations of that mechanistic concept of what human life is about. There is something in me that has always rejected them or held back.

And what I suppose I've got to recognize now is that, for as long as I can remember, I have had at the core of my life a religious conviction, because that is, I think, what Thoreau is talking about here. I don't want to label the religious conviction. I don't think I can call myself a Christian. I don't think I am entitled to call myself anything simply because my disciplines are very, very vague at this point in my life. But I do know that I have a conviction which is exactly what Thoreau formulated for me in that paragraph.

And simply because I think it might make his statement a little bit more clear, I am going to read the lead into that paragraph. This is in fact how he gets there:

"Every morning was a cheerful invitation to make my life of equal simplicity and, I may say, innocence with nature herself. I have been as sincere a worshipper of Aurora as the Greeks. I got up early and bathed in the pond. That was a religious exercise and one of the best things which I did.

"They say that characters were engraven on the bathing tub of King Ching-Thang to this effect: 'Renew thyself completely each day. Do it again, and again, and forever again.' I can understand that. Morning brings back the heroic ages.

"I was as much affected by the faint hum of a mosquito making its invisible and unimaginable tour through my apartment at earliest dawn when I was sitting with door and windows open as I could be by any trumpet that ever sang of fame. It was Homer's requiem, itself an *Iliad* and *Odyssey* in the air, singing it's own wroth and wanderings. There was something cosmical about it, a standing advertisement, though forbidden, of the everlasting vigor and fertility of the world.

"The morning which is the most memorable season of the day is the awakening hour. Then, there is least somnolence in us, and for an hour at least some part of us awakes which slumbers all the rest of the day and night. Little is to be expected of that day, if can be called a day, to which we are not awakened by our genius, but by mechanical nudgings of some servitor, or not awakened by our own newly acquired force and aspirations from within accompanied by the undulations of celestial music instead of factory bells and a fragrance filling the air to a higher life than we fell asleep from.

"And thus, the darkness bears its fruit and proves itself to be good no less than the light. That man who does not believe that each day contains an earlier, more sacred, and auroral hour than he has yet profaned, has despaired of life and is pursuing a descending and darkening way. After a partial cessation of his sensuous life, the soul of man, or its organs rather, are re-invigorated each day, and his genius tries again that noble life it can make.

"All memorable events, I should say, transpire in a morning time and in a morning atmosphere. The Vedas say, 'All intelligences awake with the morning.' Poetry and art, and the fairest and most memorable of the actions of men date from such an hour. All poets and heroes like Memnon are the children of Aurora and emit their music at the sunrise. To him whose elastic and vigorous thought keeps pace with the sun, the day is a perpetual morning. It matters not what the clocks say or the attitudes and labors of men. Morning is when I am awake, and there is a dawn in me.

"Moral reform is effort to throw off sleep. Why is it that men give so poor an account of their day if they have not been slumbering? They are not such poor calculators. If they have not been overcome with drowsiness, they would have performed something. The millions are awake enough for physical labor, but only one in a million is awake enough for effective intellectual exertion; only one in 100 million to a poetic or divine life.

"To be awake is to be alive, and I have never yet met a man who was quite awake. How could I have ever looked him in the face. We must learn to re-awaken and keep ourselves awake, not by mechanical aids, but by an infinite expectation of the dawn which does not forsake us in our soundest sleep. I know of no more encouraging fact than the unquestioned ability of man to elevate his life by a conscious endeavor. It is something to be able to paint a particular picture, or carve a statue, and so to make a few objects beautiful. But it is far more glorious to carve and paint the very atmosphere and medium through which we look which morally we can do. To affect the quality of the day, that is the highest of arts."

I don't think we can weaken what Thoreau has said in those sentences and that page, or try to deny the challenge by saying that he lived in a simpler time, that the issues he faced in his little cabin beside the Walden Pond in a rustic New England 170 years ago were primitive by comparison with what we have to wrestle with. It is true that his penny postage has been replaced by our FAX machines, and that our technology has complicated our lives beyond anything he could possibly have conceived of when he wrote those lines.

But I am prepared to stick my neck out and say that those five men who went into orbit yesterday, that extraordinary and very impressive and beautiful, magnificent achievement, that those men with that unbelievably sophisticated technology that carried them into space which they have been dealing with, using, putting payloads in orbit, is that I don't think they carry with them one piece of moral or ethical equipment that Thoreau didn't have at his disposal beside Walden Pond.

I hope that what I have said to you indicates what for me now is a really rock solid faith in the ability of a human being, any human being, to make progress towards his or her personal salvation in whatever terms you choose. I know it's true, because it is part of my experience now. I actively work at it, and I know you can move. You can move your life.

I must balance that, however, by saying that I find myself becoming increasingly pessimistic about our social experiments. I don't know that we're doing a good job of managing this earth that we live on. I am still appalled by the fact that in a presidential debate a week ago, apart from one quip at the state of Boston Harbor, not one of the candidates addressed himself with any sense of urgency or gravity to the question of what we are doing to the earth.

I make this rather pessimistic point, simply because this wonderful book wouldn't have been written and be there for us had Thoreau found the world in which we find ourselves. I know that instances can be cited where we have been able to reverse the pattern of events, but I don't think they hold out any real comfort actually. I think the cleaning up of one toxic waste site when we've created another 10 on the same day, the rehabilitation of the mountain gorilla in one corner of Zaire when maybe 100 species of different animals and plants have been lost in the Amazon River Basin, I think our progress towards some sort of terrible catastrophe is kind of inevitable as I read it. That's the scenario I imagine. And one just hopes that when it finally catches up with us, there will be enough of the moral quality that Thoreau wrote about in the survivors possibly to help us start again and begin anew.

Q: *Could you assume that technology then is a force that works against creativity?*

DR. FUGARD: No. I don't know that we've learnt how to couple it. I think it has outstripped us. In itself, there is absolutely nothing wrong with it. Technology is a tool. Would you agree with that as an essential statement?

And I don't think there is anything wrong with any tool. It is a question whether we know how to use it. I think that we are discussing something that could well bring the world which we know to its knees. I think man has not put as much time into what Thoreau talks about as he has into technology. We have, perhaps, reached the point where we know how dangerous it is. There are certain tools you just don't allow a child to play with. I think we're reaching that sort of stage where we are acquiring tools without the responsibility that should go with using them.

Let us take one simple fact: the number of hungry and starving people on this earth at this moment. We know that we have not only the stocks and the stores to eliminate hunger, but we also have the technology and the knowhow to prevent it from ever happening again. But that's not going to happen. And why is it not going to happen? Food is not going to reach certain hungry people in Ethiopia because a government in power sees them as rebels and won't allow the supplies through.

Certain other things will not happen because of the greed of corporate organizations. Our intellectual and moral development has not kept pace with our technology, and I think the consequences are patently obvious. The earth cannot sustain any more a situation which we ourselves cannot manage, and I do not think any of our social tools are helping us very much.

I am not criticizing technology at all; I think it's extraordinary. I know, however, that I would be a very much better human being if I did something about the degree to which I pollute my life even just psychologically by way of noise. I do not have a discipline which gives me a period of silence every day of my life—a period of personal reflection.

I can remember the last occasion I came to Georgetown University. I spent a wonderful evening at dinner with Father Healy and friends, and Father Healy was very challenging at the end of that evening. He spoke to those of us who were visitors, and he said, "Throw out a few provocations to me in terms of what I should do about the young people who come to this establishment." And I can remember saying to him, "You know, silence; just that, silence. The book wouldn't have been written without silence."

Now, I don't think this a passing, or just a negative issue; I think it's absolutely critical. The fact that greed is cultivated and has been made socially acceptable; that greed for power and material wealth has been established and put on a pedestal as a totally socially accepted motivation is very dangerous. I thought that every significant religion warned that power was very dangerous.

Anyway, I don't want to get sidetracked. Thank you.

Q: *Do you believe we are prepared to take up the challenge of restoring our environment yet?*

DR. FUGARD: No. I think we've got to try, but I don't think the attempts are being made in the right direction, at the correct level. For example, I mentioned that two candidates for presidency of the

United States debated publicly a week ago, and in the course of that debate, they listed an agenda of very important issues. One of them was not what we are going to do about the physical world in which we are living now. Now, I've got to ask myself, "Did they not take on that issue and are they not prepared to speak out in as dramatic, forceful, and final terms as are required simply because big money is behind them, and that they would alienate big money?"

Because you must understand, to get our world right a lot of people are going to have to make sacrifices, and we are going to have to make the most. At this point, I think if those sacrifices were clearly spelled out, people would say no. If it were fully realized the personal sacrifices in living standards that we need to make in order to get our world really back on its feet again and to make our relationship to it viable, most of us would refuse.

Since the human experiment began on the face of the earth, there have only been a handful of cultures which were able to integrate themselves into the environment to such an extent that they weren't violent and disruptive; that they, in fact, became part of a cycle of renewal, of constant renewal. I know that, for example, in my own country, the Koi-san people, the Bushmen, were a magnificent example of a culture of people that were so integrated into the natural pattern and order of life that they were not involved in progressive destruction of the environment.

By and large, the history of man in terms of all the other cultures has been one of progressive destruction and depletion of the environment. I don't say that we are incapable of finding a viable solution or making a move towards it. I just don't believe that we will do so, until we really find ourselves in very serious trouble. Because of personal greed, and because of the costs involved, and because of the self-sacrifice needed, I do not believe that we will do it. It will require us landing up in very serious trouble before the efforts finally are made.

Q: What do you believe we should look for in our leaders morally?

DR. FUGARD: This is where I begin to get pessimistic, because I think the man who decided to be really honest, really address the issue, would not get the backing he needed to advance politically. I think politics and big money are now inseparably tied together. Now that is the bad news! I don't believe that we have got a situation any more where one man can make a difference politically. There are other arenas of action and of human endeavor and effort where that is not the case, but in terms of politics, in terms of finally being in the White House, I think one is in the situation, which is no different in other countries, where politics means money and profit, and profit means scant regard, for example, for the renewal of forests which are being logged out of existence. Certainly, the big factories that are producing more waste, dangerous waste, than we can deal with are not going to be closed down. I do not think that any man who stood up and said those things would be a viable candidate in an American election. That is why I say my thinking is tinged with pessimism on the score of the big social experiment, though not as regards individual endeavor. We know, thanks to the writings of extraordinary men and women, that even in the nightmare of an Auschwitz, or a Belsen, or a Buchenwald, individual human beings worked at their salvation and achieved it, or at least, made progress towards it. It is extraordinary what the individual human spirit can do. And I know from my own country, South Africa, where there is a conspiracy to brutalize, and mutilate, and diminish, and deprive the lives of people simply by virtue of their skin color, the extraordinary fact that there are men and women who have not allowed that system to stop them in their individual journey towards being a better human being. In fact, that was the very special challenge I realized about Thoreau's words that night in Johannesburg. I don't think it was just a ploy on the part of a guilt-stricken, liberal, white conscience to lessen my sense of responsibility. When I read those words that night, I said to myself—it was a very hard and challenging thing to say to myself—"These words of his have got to be just as true for me in the safety and comfort of this hotel room, must be as true for a black man or woman, hungry, shivering out in the freezing cold of that Johannesburg winter's night, huddled on a park bench, because there was nowhere else for their truth to come alive. These words have got to be as true for you, black brother, in your misery as they are for me in my comfort." That's a hard one, but I've got to believe it.

Q: In his acceptance speech for the Nobel Prize For Literature, William Faulkner said that the will of man was not merely to endure, but to prevail, and that it was the work of the writer to be a pillar to help him prevail."

I'm curious as to how—in the nature of your work and the way that you've spent your life—you feel that as a writer you have helped man not merely to endure, but to prevail?

DR. FUGARD: If I have done that, it is because in everything that I have ever written, at the core of my intention in telling any of the stories I have told, has been a desire to make an affirmation about the human spirit and the fact that it can prevail. Now, whether that has been a story—as in *Master Harold*—about a white boy and two black friends, or the play that I have just done, I have tried to bear witness to what I see as a capacity in the human spirit in certain people for being indomitable even in the face of the most terrible threats either from within themselves, or from without. Because this is the point again, an aspect of what I've tried to say today, that there are two levels of victimization in the course of living a life. You can be the victim of forces bigger than yourself, almost beyond your control, as is the case in South Africa if you happen to be born with a black skin. You are a victim of a racist state. You can also be a victim of yourself, and I have tried in my storytelling, as a playwright, to break the bondage of both sorts of victimizations.

Q: Dr. Fugard, you said this morning that you wanted to speak to us both reservedly and thoughtfully, and I think you've not only spoken in that manner, but it strikes me that you've lived in that manner also, and I admire that. What I wanted to ask you was, when you said those words, reservedly and thoughtfully, it reminded me immediately of Thoreau's words in giving his reasons for wanting to live in the woods at Walden. He said that he went "in order to learn how to live more deliberately." Could you give some interpretation to us of what you think he may have meant by the words "learning to live deliberately?"

DR. FUGARD: I love the quote—I can't put my hand on it immediately—but there is a quote somewhere else in *Walden* where Thoreau says that his intention was to set himself up in this little shack and live life as simply as he could, because he wanted to corner it. He said he wanted to get it into a corner, so that he could subject it to the most thorough examination he was capable of, and if it was a sham and a fraud and not worth it, to announce that very loudly, and if the converse proved to be the case, to announce that very loudly as well.

Thank God he did it. And obviously, the conclusion he came to was that life was worth living.

Q: Dr. Fugard, this morning you have spoken about the human rights abuses in South Africa. It is evident to me today that, in order to make the world a better place for everyone, to make the world a decent place for everyone and not just the lucky few, we not only have to elevate our own souls, as

Thoreau would have said, but elevate the souls of others. What would Thoreau have said to this problem which is inherent, I think, in the situation of the world today? Would Thoreau make any suggestions if he were here today about how to help other people to rise?

DR. FUGARD: What I'll do is put it in a nutshell, because that remains a passionate conviction of mine. I'll put in a nutshell something I really, really believe with every fiber of my being. Again, part of this great conspiracy, or rather one of the forces conspiring—because there is no evil genius—to make the individual feel impotent is this sense that unless you have an audience of 100 million people, what effect can you have? Unless you are a presidential candidate up against another presidential candidate, what effect can you have?

Now, I believe there is an arena of action in life vastly more important than any of the arenas that people commonly think of as the place where things happen, and the arena I am talking about is where one man or woman addresses himself or herself to another man or woman. The one-on-one arena of our daily lives is, I think, central to history.

You see, we have a very, very shallow conception in this day and age of what human action, and the consequences of human action, are about. We treat human action rather the way we treat coffee, or the lottery. It's got to be instant. We have completely lost the sense of the mystery about human action, the way you can do something in life and how consequences of that action can move so mysteriously, and how it might not be at that precise moment that you get your return. It might not even be tomorrow. But I don't know. Our sense of acting and doing has become so shallow. We have lost so much faith in reaching out and touching one other human being. I think what we really need to do is rediscover a powerful faith in that mystery, in just what one is going to do with the rest of the day, and how one is going to deal with whomever crosses one's path today. I think that there you've already got the answer to your question.

I think we immediately jump to the conclusion that we've got to find some vast action to reach out, and obviously there is that sense as well in regard to our relation to the people in Cambodia, to the people in my country. How do we affect their circumstances? Well, I think you start with giving your utmost seriousness to the arena of your own life, to the rights and wrongs that come your way today.

Q: Dr. Fugard, many critics would accuse Thoreau of some sort of escapism and that somehow he is really running away from the world man has created, society. First of all, do you think he really did escape totally from society living in a cabin at Walden Pond, and if he did, what message does this give to the world? I mean, if the world is like a house on fire, has he just let it continue to burn if he's in that cabin, or is he in some way going to change that?

DR. FUGARD: I don't think Thoreau really escaped from human society. I mean, there are other recorded examples of people who have really, really done that. I don't think Thoreau's escape was an escape from society.

What I think Thoreau did was to try to make his life as simple as possible. Within himself, he didn't leave the company of men and live totally, in the sense that a hermit or a sage makes a complete and total active withdrawal, as in some religions, particularly those in the East. I think that what Thoreau did was simplify his life as radically as he could, so that he could better understand what the rock bottom values were. As I tried to say earlier, I think that what he finally understood and discovered as being the rock bottom values are very much the same today for us as they were for him.

Q: Dr. Fugard, it appears that all over the world in all different nations people are moving, the peasants are moving from the country to the city, and they're leaving behind their heritage and their culture. Do you think that we should try to resuscitate these cultures, or do you think that, given the situation, it's almost more important that we assimilate these people into the world in which they have to live in order to survive?

DR. FUGARD: I don't think there is any going back, and I think I can say that with a small measure of authority simply because I come from a country where what you have just described is a very massive reality in our day-to-day lives and at every level of our existence. I do not think there is any going back. I think this whole notion of the global society, or the global village, is an inescapable reality. I think there is a blueprint which we haven't drawn up yet for the future which is going to involve a restructuring of society in a way I don't think we have any real understanding of yet. But going back is, I think, pointless. It would be retrograde. I don't think there is any salvaging anything of that. Thank you.

KEVIN M. CAHILL, M.D.

ON

"The Collected Poems" of William Butler Yeats

What they undertook to do
They brought to pass;
All things hang like a drop of dew
Upon a blade of grass.

"Gratitude To The Unknown Instructors,"
W. B. YEATS

As we gather to celebrate the Bicentennial of this university, its leaders ask us to reflect on liberal education, human excellence, and classic texts. They ask us to consider how we have grown within an academic tradition which taught us to draw from, and maybe even add to, that special body of literature that shapes our youthful dreams, encourages mature aspirations, and replenishes, over and over again, the spirit that struggles for integrity, purpose, and sometimes even survival in a system that too often seems to reward only mediocrity and conformity. President Healy suggests that we provide a focus to this exercise by selecting a single book from a lifetime's readings.

My text was not hard to find. A well-worn volume, it lay by my bedside, as it has since it was given to me—as the inscription by my father reminds me—when I was twelve. It's been alongside me since then wherever I've been, through college and medical school, through the pivotal period as a young Navy physician in Africa, through courtship and marriage and the birth of our sons, in good times and bad, through all the years that sometimes now can seem

From our birthday until we die
Is but the winking of an eye.

I come before you as the product of a Jesuit education, but one, as I shall try to explain, that began in infancy, was influenced in childhood by the orations and idiosyncratic logic of my father, who often transferred his Regis, Fordham, and Georgetown views of the world to his offspring through the medium of poetry. My own university years at Rose Hill added a bit of polish to that familial foundation.

Now most new knowledge that flows, or trickles, into the reservoir of my learning comes primarily from my sons who, happily, carry home—and on to their secular universities and lives—Regis and Loyola influences that, at least to their grateful parents, seem beneficially formative. Not everyone has viewed Jesuit education so positively, and it might be well, as we begin this Bicentennial weekend, inundated, I will presume, with congratulatory notes, including a message from the president of the United States, to recall that two of his predecessors in the White House did not greet the restoration of the Jesuits in the land of the free with any enthusiasm.

In 1816, John Adams wrote to Thomas Jefferson: "I do not like the resurrection of the Jesuits . . . who are more numerous than everybody knows . . . in as many shapes and disguises as ever the King of Gypsies himself assumed: in the shape of Printers, Editors, Writers, School Masters, etc. . . . if ever any Congregation of Men could merit eternal perdition on Earth and in Hell . . . it is the Company of Loyola." Had Adams employed a speech writer, he no doubt would have dubbed the Jesuits "an evil empire."

Somehow the nation survived, and thrived, along with Georgetown, the mother of a long line of Catholic colleges and universities that have played a prominent role in American intellectual life. They have provided, as has the book I have chosen, a unique view on national debates, a historical and religious perspective that allows one to find joy in sorrow and avoid, sometimes, the temptations of the latest vogue. We convene at a time in the history of our nation when fundamental questions have been raised regarding our role, not only as powerful leaders in an increasingly divided world but as fellow human beings who share a single planet and a finite time on earth.

The literary career of William Butler Yeats spans more than a half century. His *Collected Poems* offer a temporal, developmental aspect which a single text, technical or literary, cannot provide. The collection moves from the simple rhymes of childhood through the passionate poems of physical desire, from the attempts to capture arcane theological theories in iambic pentameter to single, memorable lines that distill the universal experiences of combat and confusion, rejection and despair, and lead, ultimately, to a wisdom that has been a source of strength and courage at different stages of my life.

I begin my reflections on *The Collected Poems* with two cautions. Yeats, like the rest of us, was far from perfect, and—at times—as wrong-headed as a person can be. One does not read poetry to support a thesis or buttress an argument as one might utilize journals in preparing a scientific paper. To draw solace and inspiration from Yeats's poems does not mean that one must accept his entire philosophy. His ideas were not always admirable and sometimes were even despicable. It would be difficult, for instance, even to attempt to defend Yeats's period of neo-Nazi Blue-shirt fascination—were it not that one can almost feel a poetic soul groping for order.

Scholars may analyze and annotate and even "deconstruct" Yeats's text but I, fortunately, am in a position to use his volume only as a basis for personal reflections. Even if I had the knowledge—which I do not—to present myself as a Yeatsian authority, I would side with the poet who wondered:

*What would they say
Did their Catullus
Talk that way?*

With those caveats in mind, I will share with you the pervasive influence of Yeats's poems on my life. I will relate an individual view of how my own liberal education and the Jesuit-inspired teachings of my father and sons fashioned my own concepts of and aspirations toward human excellence and opened my mind so that education leads not to a conclusion but to unimagined frontiers. The journey of discovery ends, hopefully, only with death, and the sense of mission we inherit—and transmit—is the great unfinished gift we celebrate in these ancient halls of learning.

CHILDHOOD

My exposure to Yeats's poems began in a Bronx Irish immigrant household where the oral tradition held sway and we truly felt sorry for those who were missing the excesses we thought normal. Oh, we probably knew, even as children, that too much alcohol was consumed, and that roast beef shouldn't always be charred, but somehow the joy of having my father recite long poems made dinnertime magic.

My earliest recollection of a Yeats poem is, probably at age four or five, hearing the lilt of his lullaby.

> *The angels are stooping*
> *Above your bed;*
> *They weary of trooping*
> *With the whimpering dead.*

And now, a generation later, as my five sons leave the nest to fashion their independent lives, I often find myself thinking of the last lines of that poem:

> *I sigh that kiss you,*
> *For I must own*
> *That I shall miss you*
> *When you have grown.*

Yeats held his place in those Sunday night festivals of love somewhere between Robert Service and Catullus, a definite notch below the Aeneid and the Odyssey which were recited, repetitively, in the Latin and Greek my father had learned from the Jesuits. The Cahills were, we were told, descendants of the High Kings of Ireland; even if the throne now apparently stood in Uncle Dinny's cold water flat in the Bronx, there was still a genetic nobility we accepted and treasured. There was an emphasis on integrity and honesty, on love and loyalty, on the need to dream of things that never were, and the willingness to openly share these fantasies with family. If Hirsch's anthropologic theory of education (in *Cultural Literacy*) is valid, then it was those early ethnic experiences that were woven, strand by oral strand, into patterns which preserved for a new generation both Cahill traditions and our distinctive means of communication.

The early years of childhood and adolescence were a privileged period of protected discovery. Particularly in a large, close family, before each member's identity emerged, one's self seemed an extension of an already existing organism. We were happy and secure in a home life that I can recall as vividly as the poet remembers Innisfree:

> *And I shall have some peace there, for peace*
>   *comes dropping slow,*
> *Dropping from the veils of the morning to where*
>   *the cricket sings;*

There midnight's all a glimmer, and noon a purple
  glow,
And evening full of linnet's wings.

Those were innocent days in a seaside town and in the undeveloped parts of the Bronx, when many roads were not yet paved and patients paid my physician father with eggs and goat's milk. It was a time—even as World War II began—of dreams:

I walk among long dappled grass,
And pluck till time and times are done
The silver apples of the moon,
The golden apples of the sun.

Our childhood instruction was not devoid of content, and academic advancement was certainly carefully monitored, but as I look back now the important lessons, the beginnings of a true liberal education, were begun in the home, not the school. There were goals and accomplishments that could not be measured with grades but were understood, even then, to be far more important than the formal academic curriculum. Somehow the liberal education that leads us into our own souls, that defines how we make judgments, and girds us for the struggles that even a child sees coming was transmitted, at least in my instance, from father to son in lines of poetry.

We learned from ballads and myths that troubled seas were an inevitable part of the journey of life. The odes and stories—as well as the foibles of innumerable relatives—made us aware, in those gentle Introductory Courses to Maturity, that not always would we "dance upon the shore" nor be bothered by "the wind or water's roar," that sooner or later we would not merely "lie long and dream in the bed/Of the matching of ribbons for bosom and head." In every good tale there came a time when "the seed of the fire flickered and grew cold," and we were taught not to fear the unknown.

Education, right from the start, should liberate not only the mind, but the heart and even the soul. Stories and examples should emphasize tolerance and expose the folly of prejudice, "for arrogance and hatred are the wares/Peddled in the thoroughfares." Becoming free and independent needs a foundation rooted in ancient myths, for even as one grows with age and experience, readings and travel, there is a baseline against which one compares new information and those first temptations of a wider world—"I knew a phoenix in my youth, so let them have their day." Even if we suspected our ties to those ancestral kings of Ireland were not quite legitimate, we learned to view, with regal disdain, titles and mere material goods, the artificial power of politicians and even "the cloth."

In a large family, immersed in Yeats, one learned to be tolerant, not "to quarrel with a thought because it was not their own," and avoid the tragic trap of calling "pleasures evil that happier days thought good." Maybe one needs the innocence and security of youth to completely believe

> *For the good are always the merry,*
> *Save by an evil chance,*
> *And the merry love the fiddle,*
> *And the merry love to dance:*

—but what a difference that view of the world makes as one prepares for sorrows, struggles, and the reality of maturity.

But most of all, in a childhood filled with Yeats and the residue of my father's Jesuit liberal education, we learned how to live and love. We learned through literature how to approach adolescence, how to reach out and appreciate the rare and unique in other people, and to treasure those "moments of glad grace," the beauty of "a pilgrim soul" and "the sorrows of a changing face." We were taught to "dream of soft looks and of shadows deep," to learn about gentleness and reverence, to begin to relate, and even compete, without violence, to understand the value and the power of words as arms for the inevitable battles to come:

> *They have spoken against you everywhere*
> *But weigh this song with the great and*
>   *their pride;*
> *I made it out of a mouthful of air,*
> *Their children's children shall say they have*
>   *lied.*

These were the lessons we took from youth, the lasting gifts of a home filled with love and passionate rhyme. Though they now are but "memories, vague memories," they remain the core and compass of my life.

UNIVERSITY DAYS

The search for self took Yeats, as it takes many of us, down paths that prove fruitless and, in retrospect, slightly embarrassing. There is dalliance with various intellectual and social fads, when every passing fancy tempts you from your chosen craft. There are obsessions with dress and style, maximalist and minimalist, reflecting both the exuberance and the tragedy that the young begin to sense in the world at large.

There are the temptations—based on false arrogance—to judge oneself superior to the hordes of plain, unlettered humanity who daily wrench an existence from life through sweat, toil, and sacrifice. Yeats, the Anglo-Irish aristocrat, noted archly at this period in his own life that his blood had not passed through "any huckster's loins," as did that of the cattle- and horse-selling, shopkeeping population he disdained in Ireland—and as did, I'll assume, the seed of most of my own immigrant forebears.

Like Yeats, most of us pass through similar phases, especially if we are blessed with the good fortune to attend a university where the privileged can convene, and blossom, in early adulthood. The elitism and mystery of fraternities and clubs, the initiation rights, and the easy assumption of superiority are almost predictable aberrations. But the early principles and values taught at home and the influence of wise professors make these aberrations difficult to sustain for too long. If we're lucky, we move on to the fuller, more fulfilling life the university offers.

This is the time when one attempts, as a twenty-three-year-old Yeats noted, "to hammer your thoughts into unity," when "the fascination of what's difficult has dried the sap out of my veins," when men wear themselves out with dreams and passions. Gradually, one takes all these experiences, lays the template of those precious lessons of childhood over them, and fashions tools for self-discovery, fulfillment, or survival.

The rewards of a humanistic education are distilled into a way of life where innocence is not lost but refined, where curiosity replaces false confidence, and where humility and modesty are understood, and a gentle and generous understanding of others' faults and gifts evolves. One learns the importance of manners

> *In courtesy I'd have her chiefly learned;*
> *Hearts are not had as a gift but hearts are*
> *earned.*

And one becomes aware of the rights and the rituals of courtship:

> *Ceremony's a name for the rich horn*
> *And custom for the spreading laurel tree.*

These are the years Georgetown celebrates, that critical stage when young men and women, for two hundred years, have come here seeking definition, fashioning an ethos, learning to inherit, from learned guides, the best from the past and preparing to transform and transmit this experience to their own and to the next generation.

Hopefully, they have learned here how to handle rejection and despair as well as happiness and success. The harsh experiences of adult life are made tolerable by the lessons of the liberal education begun in childhood and polished in the classrooms of life. It's the time of life when I began to glimpse the meaning and the wisdom—inaccessible to a child—of the lines Yeats wrote for one who had to deal with sordid and unfair causes for failure. The training of youth, the poet hoped, had bred his friend "to a better thing than triumph" and would allow him to "be secret and exult," even in defeat. The armor of a liberal education begins to shine.

It's a time when we learn, in Yeats's words, "that all is changed, changed utterly/A terrible beauty is born." The graduate must ultimately go forth from these hallowed protected halls, using all that has been stored in that "rag and bone shop of the heart," all that has been absorbed from family and teachers. He or she may find their "embroidered coat" of worldly training torn by competitors, but now the wise owners will realize that such information is but a superficial covering on the secure base of a liberal education. In fact, there may be, as we almost always come to understand, times in life when there is as much "enterprise in walking naked."

INTERNATIONAL HEALTH AND FOREIGN POLICY

All these bits and pieces of our past eventually coalesce, if we are fortunate, and prepare us for the ultimate challenges and the roles we may be unexpectedly asked to play along life's erratic pilgrimage.

Cultural and ethnic pride and themes of emerging nationalism and questions as to what constitutes patriotism permeate the poetic lines of middle-aged Yeats. He served as a senator of the Free State and spoke nobly, if unsuccessfully, in his government's debates on censorship, divorce, artistic freedom, and education. He wrote about his years in public life in his poems on "Church and State," "On Being Asked for a War Poem," and "Easter 1916." As he gained experience and insight, he gradually became disillusioned with the self-serving aspects that seem to characterize so much of what is euphemistically called "public service." He castigated the "Leaders of the Crowd":

*They must to keep their certainty accuse
All that are different of base intent;
Pull down established honor; hawk for news
Whatever their loose fantasy invent.*

And in "Nineteen Nineteen," Yeats bitterly denounced the distortion that politicians can create even from the dreams of independence:

*We, who seven years ago
Talked of honour and truth,
Shriek with pleasure if we show
The weasel's twist, the weasel's tooth.*

My own pilgrimage led from college to medical school and eventually in directions never imagined even among all the visions my father spun out of words at the dinner table in the Bronx. I am a physician who has had the good fortune to work in troubled areas of Africa, Latin America, and Asia for the past quarter century. I have seen war and revolution, earthquakes and droughts, famine and floods. I have established national health services in poverty-stricken Third World countries that had few or no doctors. For six years, I directed the most complex state medical system in the United States. Yeats captured in a few lines why I entered, and continue to find great satisfaction in, public health among the poorest.

*The wrong of unshapely things is a wrong too
    great to be told;
I hunger to build them anew and sit on a green
    knoll apart....*

C.P. Snow once wrote (in *Science and Government*) "No one that I have read has found the right answers. Very few have even asked the right questions. The best I can do is tell a story." To respond to the initial question President Healy asked in inviting me to this convocation—"Why do you do the things you do?"—I shall try, with stories of two tropical areas, to link that liberal education I have described to the unusual challenges my professional career has offered. These experiences may strike a resonant note in your minds or—even better—a dissonant one that will lead to lively discussion.

Along the way, it will be clear—I hope—how rereading the poems of Yeats has continued to offer guidance that is frequently more effective than all the knowledge and training I acquired in medical school.

THE SUDAN

I once ran a clinic in Fashoda, eight hundred miles south of Khartoum, where Marchand and Kitchener held their momentous meeting that carved up the colonial map, and the lives, of modern Africans. No one consulted the "natives"—they were naked, primitive, and couldn't speak our language and didn't, until they were forced to, worship our God. But one only worked among the Shilluk and Nuer and Dinka for a short time before one realized they had retained their ancient crafts and understood the ways of the river and the beauty of the swamps better than the white man could imagine.

Because the missionaries were ejected from the southern Sudan while I was there in the early sixties, I found myself as the only physician within hundreds of miles in any direction. There were no courses in medical school that prepared one for these challenges, for understanding that pride and tradition and culture were as essential as aspirin or bandages in running a rural medical program.

One comes to realize that prejudice and economic exploitation are realities that must be faced—and openly attacked—if one is to fulfill the obligations of the physician. It is necessary to appreciate the cry of the oppressed and the burden of ignorance, fear, and poverty if one is to practice medicine in a developing land, especially during periods of chaos and disaster. There had been no lectures in the medical school curriculum that would help me establish refugee camps or deal with a system where cultural influences made it difficult, if not impossible, for nurses to care for the opposite sex. Our training in diagnosis and therapy had prepared one for the well-stocked consulting room, but not for the grand scale that I now faced.

I discovered that politics, prejudice, racism, religion, weather, and witchcraft were integral parts of most of the medical problems I had to deal with, and solutions were discovered more frequently in those Jesuit lectures on Aristotelian logic and Thomistic reasoning, on an understanding and humility first fostered in courses in comparative religion and in the bitter lessons of history, even if one came to realize that most of the history we had learned was biased to glorify Western achievements.

I had never considered how to construct a health service with few supplies and only semi-skilled "dressers" in the middle of a war zone. The "witch doctor" had a hold on the community but his results left much to be desired. Does one fight such a system using the formidable forces of science and technology, or should one accommodate by abandoning that superior perch we have built from knowledge and training, in order to serve the suffering? I saw no alternative and we joined forces. He helped get me people to train and spread the word that my modern methods complemented his insights and skills.

There were experiences that tested the very core of a young doctor's soul. I recall staying up the first few nights after the missionary families and their followers fled. They had staffed the local hospital and dispensed all medical care for an area that could cover the whole northeastern United States. I would deliver babies and sew up animal bites, try to dress fetid wounds and even amputate gangrenous limbs. But finally, exhausted, I said I was going to sleep and I did. They called me shortly thereafter to say a woman was bleeding and I got up to help and then returned to bed. And again they called and I refused to get up. I said I couldn't survive if I didn't sleep and sent them away and I slept soundly for ten hours.

I don't know to this day what ingredients—apart from sheer exhaustion—led to that decision. But looking back, I'm sure that somewhere amid all the nuances the Jesuits had taught me about facing such ethical and moral dilemmas, I remembered the lines of Yeats:

Too long a sacrifice
Can make a stone of the heart.

At any rate, I began a daily routine of hard work, during the day organizing a basic health service, sharing the satisfying credit with my "witch-doctor" friend, training volunteers in first-aid, and going to sleep at night after a decent dinner of gazelle or quail. I stayed for months in the southern Sudan and almost felt guilty realizing how much I enjoyed this bizarre experience. None of the doctors who replaced me stayed very long because they did not believe it was moral to leave the dying and go to bed. They felt that violated their Hippocratic oath, and would work nobly till they fell, which they usually did in a matter of days.

The program collapsed, the modern medical men went back to their laboratories and clinics, and the indigenous people to their own methods of survival. That experience was over twenty-five years ago, and civil war in the southern Sudan today poses the same dilemma for a young physician who might find himself or herself there. What to do, how, why? Interesting questions, I think, for a community like Georgetown to consider as it ponders the uses of a humanistic education.

Humility and wisdom come slowly, especially in a profession accustomed to praise. It takes time—and intimate experience—with "things uncomely and broken, all things worn out and old" to balance the romance of youth, to change the passion of love into caring and compassion. It is certainly safer to reap the rewards and stay within the expected confines of a medical career but that was not what fate offered nor, it seemed to me, what the lessons of a liberal education demanded. Yeats noted that the parched tree of freedom is not watered by "polite meaningless words" but by that "excess of love" we had inherited in an immigrant home and honed in a Jesuit university.

NICARAGUA

Medicine has allowed me to function in that fascinating interface where death and life coexist. I have come to appreciate, if not always fully understand, the multiple forces that influence human—and medical—reactions. Ideally, compassion and generosity are not merely individual traits; somehow a great nation—and as Americans we were taught that our good fortune and hard work had offered that global destiny—should fuse those personal qualities into national policies. I had been taught that my role as a citizen was to participate to the fullest extent possible in translating the dreams of our Founding Fathers into programs that would serve those less fortunate. That was also the essence of our theology courses, and philosophy professors promoted the necessary freedom of thought so we could—and would—pursue excellence wherever that search led.

At certain times in history one must move beyond theory and dialectics. Mere acquiescence with the status quo can be as great a sin as an evil act of commission. Our liberal education not only gives us the capacity but the obligation to speak out against wrongs and argue for the oppressed. One can visit any hospital in Nicaragua today and see the effects of current policies perpetrated in the name of the American people. Mercenaries, completely funded by the United States, mine harbors, rape and kill in the name of democracy. To protect our great land from the threat of an impoverished nation, we have instituted economic embargoes that prevent the most basic health care from reaching malnourished Nicaraguan civilians. There is nothing subtle about seeing a surgical operation done without anaesthesia or watching a woman or baby strangle to death because spare parts for American-built respirators and incubators can no longer be purchased.

Are we to be merely bemused when the name of the land we love is soiled by those whose major obsession, anticommunism, is used to justify any sordid means? How does one deal with those who find it easier to violate than to heal, who employ deceit and semantic fantasies to cover their folly? As Yeats asked:

> *For how can you compete,*
> *Being honour bred, with one*
> *Who, were it proved he lies,*
> *Were neither shamed in his own*
> *Nor in his neighbors' eyes?*

One does not have the privilege of silence if one seeks the answer in a Managua hospital.

Unfortunately, our TV leaders, the blow-dried politicians on one-day tropical tours, never smell the gangrenous limbs or feel the feverish head of a dying child. Their airport interviews and pompous pronouncements are devoid of the humility—and shame—that come from firsthand experience in any clinic or ward. Yeats understood the tragedy that ideologues impose, the chaos that flows from policies built on fear and hatred, on continuing economic exploitation and the arrogant assumption that any nation—ours included—has a monopoly on wisdom or a divine right to dictate to others trying to regain their almost forgotten identity. He wrote how

> *Things fall apart; the center will not hold*
> *Mere anarchy is loosed upon the world*

and he warned that

> *The best lack all conviction while the worst*
> *Are full of passionate intensity.*

I have tried to capture in recent books some of my anger at missed opportunities, and have offered a direct response to those who confuse power with oppression. I fully realized my positions might well be unpopular with the privileged few who presume to shape our foreign policy. But it required little courage to identify with those who suffer and die in the man-made hell we have created in Nicaragua.

CONCLUSION

In honor of the two hundredth anniversary of a great university and in response to the fascinating challenge to select a single text and reflect on the relationship between liberal education and human excellence, I have, with much pleasure, returned to the Yeats that thrilled me when first I heard it recited by my father, that inspired me when I was young, helped me in courtship and in learning to love, gave me the courage to make decisions in my professional career when there were few—or no—precedents on which to base actions. His words have also sustained me during those inevitable periods of rejection and apparent defeat.

At the end of his long poetic career, Yeats left one final gift, a revised order for his *Last Poems*. Rather than conclude with the cryptic lines carved on his tombstone,

> Cast a cold eye
> On life, on Death
> Horseman, pass by!

he chose, as his ultimate statement, the poem, "Politics."

In it Yeats captures, in memorable couplets, themes that have profoundly affected me and which I raised for your consideration today. With the wisdom of age, the poet suggests a perspective that includes a healthy skepticism of worldly titles and the trappings of power. He focuses, rather, on the priority of memory and, most importantly, stresses the eternal, recreating force of love in the wondrous cycle of life:

> *How can I, that girl standing there,*
> *My attention fix*
> *On Roman or on Russian*
> *Or on Spanish politics?*
> *Yet here's a travelled man that knows*
> *What he talks about,*
> *And there's a politician*
> *That has read and thought,*
> *And maybe what they say is true*
> *Of war and war's alarms,*
> *But O that I were young again*
> *And held her in my arms.*

I am grateful to the Georgetown family for inviting me to join in your celebration and thank all of you for being here and sharing in this journey of discovery.

WILLIAM H. GRAY

ON

Martin Luther King's Why We Can't Wait

Let me begin by describing for you the time, the scene, and the setting of the work I have selected, *Why We Can't Wait*, by Martin Luther King, Jr. The book was written in a time of social upheaval in the United States; it was a time of great change. It was a time when one could see constantly on television demonstrations of black and white Americans in the South, in the United States of America, marching, praying, often being beaten, trying to dramatize the need for the change in America's public policy. This was a time when, in our own country, we segregated people based upon their race. It was also a period when many people of good will, and especially black Americans, began to challenge that public policy across the nation known as segregation. The leader of the opposition was Martin Luther King, Jr.

Every evening on television one could see dogs, see policemen beating on elderly women, young children, who were marching for their human rights here in the United States. And of course, there were many voices that were saying to those who were the demonstrators, "Why are you causing conflict and pain in America? Why are you agitating?" Many who criticized the marches accused those who were demonstrating in a non-violent way for their civil rights, hoping to have all of the opportunities that all Americans had, of being Communist agitators because certainly this was not the American way.

But one must recognize that, at that time, unlike today, black Americans did not have the guaranteed right to vote nor did they have the right to appear in many public institutions, such as hotels. In those days if you traveled to Atlanta, you didn't stay at the Holiday Inn, or Day's Inn, or the Hyatt, or the Weston, but you drove all night until you came to someplace where you knew someone. Why? Because black Americans could not stay in hotels. Fundamental rights that we all take for granted today were denied at every point, and at that time, in the late '50s and early '60s, black Americans along with whites of good will rose up and began to protest segregation, the system of legalized racism. The leader was Martin Luther King, Jr. who wrote *Why We Can't Wait* as an answer to those who said, "Civil disobedience is wrong. It is wrong to protest in this manner, such as sitting-in in restaurants, such as marching and holding rallies. It is wrong to agitate in this way. We must allow these rights and privileges to evolve, and in time they will evolve if you but be patient."

The impact of the book upon many of us was overwhelming, and the reason was because the book spoke not only to the question of whether black Americans and whites of good will should agitate and produce confrontation in order to change public policy, but it spoke to a deeper need within the body politic of this country. It spoke not only to the question of why there ought to be civil disobedience in a non-violent way, but it also spoke to the fundamental question of the rights of human beings in a democracy. It spoke to the Constitution and to the ideals and the principles that all Americans supposedly at that time pledged their allegiance to. King addressed not only the question of blacks having full rights in America, but also the question of blacks being equal partners in the human drama. And thus, the impact for many of us who had lived through the days of segregation, the impact for young blacks who had confronted segregation and who had seen the signs that said "Whites Only," "Coloreds," "Negroes," or "Niggers" who were searching for their somebodyness in a hostile environment, this work became therapeutic: it became good medicine in order to strengthen those who wanted to fight for human dignity.

The structure of the book consisted of a look back at the history of the black struggle in America, the Negro revolution—why 1963 was the first chapter—and then a look toward the question of non-violent civil disobedience, "the sword that heals."

King focused on what was a cancerous sore in the American mind, "Bull" Connors' Birmingham. And for those of you who may not know, "Bull" Connors was the Sheriff and Police Chief of the City of Birmingham. He was the head of law enforcement in that southern city where there had been one of the major confrontations, and people all over America had seen Connors on the news at work with his law enforcement agency. The third chapter focused on "Bull" Connors' Birmingham, which really could have been any southern town or city. It could have been Dallas; it could have been Montgomery; it could have been Houston; it could have been Savannah; it could have been Charleston; it could have been Raleigh-Durham,

Chapel Hill, Jacksonville, St. Augustine; it could have been any of a score of other southern cities. It focused upon the daily ravages of racism and the dehumanization that comes with it in our society. And then, it focused in the next chapter on "The New Day in Birmingham," pointing to the forces that were coming together, blacks and whites of good will seeking to change that city.

Perhaps the most famous chapter of all was "The Letter from a Birmingham Jail." This was a document written by King in response to a number of clergy who had sent him a public letter asking him to desist from public agitation, to stop the confrontation, to stop the marches. They called upon him in the name of God, as a fellow minister of the gospel, to stop doing these things that clearly were not of God. He received the letter when he was in jail, and he wrote a response which has become, I believe, a classic; this letter from a Birmingham jail, became one of the chapters in *Why We Can't Wait*.

Then, the book has a chapter on "Black and White Together" that addresses the need for integration as a goal of our society. It spoke to the urban discontent, "The Summer of Discontent." Finally, King looked into the future in terms of "The Days to Come." That was the structure of *Why We Can't Wait*. But what was the major theme?

The major theme in that book was simply a call for black Americans and for white Americans to recognize, first, that we could change America, and second, that in 1963 on the occasion of the 100th anniversary of the Emancipation Proclamation, we ought to fulfill the dream of the Constitution, of the Bill of Rights, of the 13th, 14th, and 15th Amendments, and even of the Emancipation itself. And so Martin's theme was basically a call to people of good will to join in non-violent, direct action. Influenced by Gandhi and Thoreau, he said:

> "Non-violence is a powerful and just weapon. It is a weapon unique in history which cuts without wounding, and ennobles the man who wields it. It is a sword that heals. Both a practical and a moral answer to the Negro's cry for justice, non-violent, direct action proved that it could win victories without losing wars, and so became the triumphant tactic of the Negro revolution of 1963."

Those were the words of Martin, who came forth with a unique tactic, a tactic that challenged the nation, put the issue of racism and segregation before the nation, but did it in such a way that one could not lose sight of the essential problem of racism. Often in the history of the struggle for liberation, those who were scarred and injured resorted to tactics that led to physical confrontation—riots, beatings, revenge—so the focus became the violence, and whether that was right or wrong, and everyone lost sight of the initial cause of the violence. The genius of King was the development of the tactic of non-violent, civil disobedience, where the focus remained on the issue of racism, and thus confronted the oppressor, so that if the oppressor beat you and locked you up, he lost. And if he did nothing, he lost. Thus, the oppressor was forced to face the challenge of the issue of racism and change.

So the major call of *Why We Can't Wait* was a call for non-violent, direct action, but it also recognized that if black and white America was to live up to its dream of all people having their rights, tokenism could not succeed. Evolutionary approaches to public policy would not work. One could not see an injustice and say, "Through evolution it will work out," because that was not the record of history from Martin's point of view. And thus to those who said, "Wait, Dr. King. Take it easy. We are moving toward a more perfect union," his response to such tokenism was:

> "As I write at the end of the first long season of revolution, the Negro is not mindful of or indifferent to the progress that has already been made. He notes with approval the radical change in the administration's approach to civil rights (the Kennedy administration), and the small but visible gains being made on various fronts across the country. If he is still saying, 'not enough,' it is because he doesn't feel that he should be expected to be grateful for the halting and inadequate attempts of his society to catch up with the basic rights he ought to have inherited automatically centuries ago by virtue of his membership in the human family and his American birthright."

There is the key to understanding the call. There is the key to understanding why you should not wait, why you should not depend on the evolutionary process. For Martin the issue was not simply political or economic. It was rooted more firmly in theological ground. Blacks were part of the human race, and as such, they were entitled to certain rights and privileges, which are non-debatable. "We hold these truths to be self-evident. . . ."—firmly rooted in America's own tradition. And so in a sense, what Martin did like no one else ever did was to dramatize the fact that we were basically denying, through racism and segregation the humanity of a large segment of our citizenry, and then on top of that, we also denied those people the birthright of all American citizens. This theme runs throughout *Why We Can't Wait*, and when it was articulated with its theological ground, as well as its constitutional reality, more and more people across the country began to question, "Why are we asking people to wait to be human, to be whole citizens?" This question was appropriate because, although blacks had served in every war, they still experienced legal barriers that prevented them from enjoying their basic rights and denied their humanity, a condition that we immigrants did not have to endure. This group of Americans had been here even before the Mayflower. And so Martin's call for a community that did not wait became a reality; a community that understood that there were certain laws that ought to be publicly challenged on theological and moral grounds.

He responded to those who said, "Why are you breaking the law?" He said, "The answer lies in the fact that there are two types of laws, just and unjust, and I would be the first to advocate obeying just laws. One has not only a legal, but a moral responsibility to obey just laws. Conversely, one has a moral responsibility to disobey unjust laws. I would agree with St. Augustine that an unjust law is no law at all." If you understand Martin, you understand him for what he was first and foremost: a preacher who saw the need for equal rights rooted in divine law.

King not only pricked the nation's conscience with *Why We Can't Wait*, but he also became a role model for a generation of black and white Americans. His book had a significant impact upon my life, and I believe it is a classic. It is a classic like anything from Socrates, Aristotle, or anyone else, because I think that as you look back over the landscape of the 20th century, and you look for those mountain peaks, Martin Luther King stands out as one of the foremost spiritual geniuses of our time, a man who changed this nation through his thoughts, through his ideas, and through his faith, and through a tactic of non-violence.

More importantly, he also taught a group of us that public policy can be changed, and that, even if you don't have the right to vote, you can register your concern, for ultimately, the civil rights movement was the political rights movement. Yes. It was public policy. Those of us who participated in it didn't do it by going to vote for President or members of Congress. We did it by marching, by sitting in, by praying, and sometimes dying, so that in 1964 the Public Accommodations Act was passed, and in 1965 the Voting Rights Act.

The impact of the book *Why We Can't Wait* upon my life, I think, was both deep and profound. Like any black growing up in America in the '50s and early '60s who saw the dehumanization of segregation and racism, I often asked myself, "Why? Why did this happen to me? Why did it happen to my family? Why did it happen to my mother and father? Why did people treat us this way?"

King gave us an answer; he gave us an answer that gave us hope, that allowed us to continue to struggle, but he also gave a tactic that changed public policy. I knew Martin Luther King not just as the author of *Why We Can't Wait*, but I knew him as a friend.

I first met Martin when he was a young man in Atlanta at Morehouse College. Our families were friends. My father a Baptist preacher; his father a Baptist preacher. I got to know him better when he went to Crozier Theological Seminary near Philadelphia, Pennsylvania, and I suppose like all parents did in those days and perhaps do today, they say, "Look. When you go to Georgetown, over in Alexandria, Virginia there are the Joneses, and if you need anything, call them up. You want a good home-cooked meal, or you get tired of that dormitory, go by and see them."

King, as a seminarian, used to come to our home sometimes and have dinner and also worship at our church in North Philadelphia. During those times, he was just another young student studying—a black American from a proud family with a proud heritage. No one ever suspected that underneath that exterior was a Nobel Peace Prize winner, was a man who was destined to change America and its public policy.

Thus, for me *Why We Can't Wait* was not just a classic text that helped to guide me toward a career of ministry and public policy, but it was also the culmination of a personal relationship and the crystallization of a man's thought whom I knew and knew well. And I think that is why many of us who were a part of that generation, who were a part of that movement, ended up in public policy—Walter Fauntroy, Andrew Young, just to mention a few. Why? First, because after the civil right struggle, there was the economic and political rights struggle which Martin understood as a part of his fundamental belief that all of us are God's children—men, women, black, white, Jews, Islamic, Christians, Catholics. And secondly, because he believed that we have a responsibility to challenge whatever is unjust and that this can be done with means which do not become unjust in and of themselves. Thank you.

Q: In 1988, there are 32 million Americans that are still living in poverty, not just black Americans, but Americans of every race. And I think that if Martin Luther King were alive today and walked around and saw that, he'd be very distressed. I remember reading that when he died, he was in the midst of planning a poor people's campaign that would be applying this non-violent philosophy on a massive campaign that would be centered here in Washington and designed to raise the public consciousness of the presence of poverty and the need to eradicate it. One of the things that he proposed was that we should have an "economic bill of rights" that would guarantee a good-paying job to anybody who couldn't get one through the private sector. In other words, if the private sector couldn't provide a good-paying job, the public sector would be legally obligated to provide one. Do you feel that that is, first, a worthy goal, and second, a realistic goal politically today?

CONGRESSMAN GRAY: You're right, and that's why I concluded by saying that the civil rights movement was a prelude to the economic and political rights movement, and Martin understood that. That is exactly why he moved from civil rights to broader issues of human rights worldwide, South Africa, Vietnam, the whole issue of war and militarism, the arms race; all these became major topics of concern in the mid-1960s, and also poverty. Martin Luther King, Jr. was not assassinated in a civil rights march. It was an economic fight. He was in Memphis, Tennessee fighting not for civil rights, but for the economic rights of sanitation workers, black and white, because he saw poverty as a crushing burden that killed the human spirit and kept people from being all that they could be. I say that to indicate that I agree with you. In his writings, King does talk about the fact that there needs to be a vigorous war against poverty, and, if you remember, during that period in the mid to the late 1960s we did launch a war on some of those issues. He believed that there should be education for everyone in this country universally; that college should be open to anyone, not just to those who had money, and that the role of government should be to make an education available to everyone who had the ability and had the desire. He promoted health care and housing, and also he was a strong advocate for what we call in public policy a full employment society. And, of course, we did see the passage of the Hawkins-Humphrey Bill, which stated a national goal of full employment. He was very articulate about the issues of poverty.

One of the things that happened in Martin's later life was that he began to understand in the late '60s before his death that many of the problems that we faced in urban areas of the north and west were quite different from the south. There were similarities, yes. There was racism. And so, he began to move away from the strategy of non-violence, civil disobedience, because how do you do that in a city like Philadelphia or New York when the issue was a little more complex. It wasn't just racism, but it was economic oppression as well that often had a racist base. And so, he was struggling with the issue of new strategies, and strikes were a part of that, and that's what he was doing in Memphis.

So, yes, he would probably say today that we can do better, that there still is too much poverty. I think on the one hand he would be very grateful about the changes that he would see, but at the same time I think he would be very disturbed by the fact that, despite our prosperity, poverty still exists in large pockets, continues to be structural, and there are many people who apparently don't seem to care.

I think he would be very upset about the census report of 3 weeks ago which said that poverty in '87 came down from '86 by .1 percent, from 13.6 to 13.5 percent. I think Martin Luther King would say, "That's not good enough." And he would particularly be very upset by the fact that in America today, despite 6 years of positive economic growth, poverty is higher than it was in 1980, or 1979, or 1975. The old adage about a rising tide lifting all boats is being changed to a rising tide lifts the big boats and swamps the little ones.

Q: How do you see yourself as a role model for young blacks?

CONGRESSMAN GRAY: I suppose I never really think about myself as a role model for "young blacks in America." I think of myself probably as a role model to three little boys who are not so little any more—Billy, Justin, and Andrew, my sons. But I suppose that what I try to do is. . . yes, am I aware of my blackness? Of course—aware of it and quite proud of it. But I don't dwell on it. I don't dwell on it, because essentially I come from a family background and a father who taught me that I was as good as anybody, and I can do whatever I want to do if I'm willing to work at it, if I have the character, the strength, and the commitment to do it.

And so, I ended up being Chairman of the Budget Committee of the United States House of Representatives, but people often say, "Well, you know, when you were running, did you ever think about the fact that you would be the first black to head a major financial committee of the United States Congress?" I said, "No. It never occurred to me." It only occurred afterwards when the news people said, "How's it feel to be the first black?" I've been black a long time.

I would say to young blacks in today's society that you have got opportunities that are unbelievable, that many in my generation did not have, but you also have challenges that are unbelievable that we did not have. I would simply say: One, commit yourself to excellence. Two, commit yourself to honesty. Three, commit yourself to other human beings. And four, and most importantly, believe in yourself. And finally, the last thing I always say is, despite the fact that we were able in the '60s to bring down the superstructure of legalized racism in America, nevertheless, there is still a lot of residue of bigotry, discrimination, and prejudice out there. So the fifth thing I'd say to black young people is understand that as a given of life, just as we had to understand segregation as a given of life. Work against it, but don't become so frustrated that you become immobile.

There is still a lot of bigotry out there. Fight it, but don't take time out and go pout on the sidelines complaining. That's the way to respond to it, and I think that was one of the things that Martin's book *Why We Can't Wait* did for so many of the blacks of the generation of the '50s and '60s; it showed that you could fight; you could fight effectively; you were somebody; you had dignity; don't give up; don't quit.

WILLIAM J. BRENNAN, JR.

ON

The Constitution of the United States: Contemporary Ratification

I am deeply grateful for the invitation to participate in the "Text and Teaching" symposium. This rare opportunity to explore classic texts with participants of such wisdom, acumen and insight as those who have preceded and will follow me to this podium is indeed exhilarating. But it is also humbling. Even to approximate the standards of excellence of these vigorous and graceful intellects is a daunting task. I am honored that you have afforded me this opportunity to try.

It will perhaps not surprise you that the text I have chosen for exploration is the amended Constitution of the United States, which, of course, entrenches the Bill of Rights and the Civil War amendments and draws sustenance from the bedrock principles of another great text, the Magna Carta. So fashioned, the Constitution embodies the aspiration to social justice, brotherhood, and human dignity that brought this nation into being. The Declaration of Independence, the Constitution and the Bill of Rights solemnly committed the United States to be a country where the dignity and rights of all persons were equal before all authority. In all candor we must concede that part of this egalitarianism in America has been more pretension than realized fact. But we are an aspiring people, a people with faith in progress. Our amended Constitution is the lodestar for our aspirations. Like every text worth reading, it is not crystalline. The phrasing is broad and the limitations of its provisions are not clearly marked. Its majestic generalities and ennobling pronouncements are both luminous and obscure. This ambiguity of course calls forth interpretation, the interaction of reader and text. The encounter with the Constitutional text has been, in many senses, my life's work.

My approach to this text may differ from the approach of other participants in this symposium to their texts. Yet such differences may themselves stimulate reflection about what it is we do when we "interpret" a text. Thus I will attempt to elucidate my approach to the text as well as my substantive interpretation.

Perhaps the foremost difference is the fact that my encounters with the constitutional text are not purely or even primarily introspective; the Constitution cannot be for me simply a contemplative haven for private moral reflection. My relation to this great text is inescapably public. That is not to say that my reading of the text is not a personal reading, only that the personal reading perforce occurs in a public context, and is open to critical scrutiny from all quarters.

The Constitution is fundamentally a public text—the monumental charter of a government and a people—and a Justice of the Supreme Court must apply it to resolve public controversies. For, from our beginnings, a most important consequence of the constitutionally created separation of powers has been the American habit, extraordinary to other democracies, of casting social, economic, philosophical and political questions in the form of law suits, in an attempt to secure ultimate resolution by the Supreme Court. In this way, important aspects of the most fundamental issues confronting our democracy may finally arrive in the Supreme Court for judicial determination. Not infrequently, these are the issues upon which contemporary society is most deeply divided. They arouse our deepest emotions. The main burden of my twenty-nine Terms on the Supreme Court has thus been to wrestle with the Constitution in this heightened public context, to draw meaning from the text in order to resolve public controversies.

Two other aspects of my relation to this text warrant mention. First, constitutional interpretation for a federal judge is, for the most part, obligatory. When litigants approach the bar of court to adjudicate a constitutional dispute, they may justifiably demand an answer. Judges cannot avoid a definitive interpretation because they feel unable to, or would prefer not to, penetrate to the full meaning of the Constitution's provisions. Unlike literary critics, judges cannot merely savor the tensions or revel in the ambiguities inhering in the text—judges must resolve them.

Second, consequences flow from a Justice's interpretation in a direct and immediate way. A judicial decision respecting the incompatibility of Jim Crow with a constitutional guarantee of equality is not simply a contemplative exercise in defining the shape of a just society. It is an order—supported by the full coercive power of the State—that the present society change in a fundamental aspect. Under such circumstances the process of deciding can be a lonely, troubling experience for fallible human beings conscious that their best may not be adequate to the challenge. We Justices are certainly aware that we are not final because we are infallible; we know that we are infallible only because we are final. One does not forget how much may depend on the decision. More than the litigants may be affected. The course of vital social, economic and political currents may be directed.

These three defining characteristics of my relation to the constitutional text—its public nature, obligatory character, and consequentialist aspect—cannot but help influence the way I read that text. When Justices interpret the Constitution they speak for their community, not for themselves alone. The act of interpretation must be undertaken with full consciousness that it is, in a very real sense, the community's interpretation that is sought. Justices are not platonic guardians appointed to wield authority according to their personal moral predelictions. Precisely because coercive force must attend any judicial decision to countermand the will of a contemporary majority, the Justices must render constitutional interpretations that are received as legitimate. The source of legitimacy is, of course, a wellspring of controversy in legal and political circles. At the core of the debate is what the late Yale Law School professor Alexander Bickel labeled "the counter-majoritarian difficulty." Our commitment to self-governance in a representative democracy must be reconciled with vesting in electorally unaccountable Justices the power to invalidate the expressed desires of representative bodies on the ground of inconsistency with higher law. Because judicial power resides in the authority to give meaning to the Constitution, the debate is really a debate about how to read the text, about constraints on what is legitimate interpretation.

There are those who find legitimacy in fidelity to what they call "the intentions of the Framers." In its most doctrinaire incarnation, this view demands that Justices discern exactly what the Framers thought about the question under consideration and simply follow that intention in resolving the case before them. It is a view that feigns self-effacing deference to the specific judgments of those who forged our original social compact. But in truth it is little more than arrogance cloaked as humility. It is arrogant to pretend that from our vantage we can guage accurately the intent of the Framers on application of principle to specific, contemporary questions. All too often, sources of potential enlightenment such as records of the ratification debates provide sparse or ambiguous evidence of the original intention. Typically, all that can be gleaned is the Framers themselves did not agree about the application or meaning of particular constitutional provisions, and hid their differences in cloaks of generality.

Indeed, it is far from clear whose intention is relevant—that of the drafters, the congressional disputants, or the ratifiers in the states?—or even whether the idea of an original intention is a coherent way of thinking about a jointly drafted document drawing its authority from a general assent of the states. And apart from the problematic nature of the sources, our distance of two centuries cannot but work as a prism refracting all we perceive. One cannot help but speculate that the chorus of lamentations calling for interpretations faithful to "original intention"—and proposing nullification of interpretations that fail this quick litmus test—must inevitably come from persons who have no familiarity with the historical record.

Perhaps most importantly, while proponents of this facile historicism justify it as a depoliticization of the judiciary, the political underpinnings of such a choice should not escape notice. A position that upholds constitutional claims only if they are within the specific contemplation of the Framers in effect establishes a presumption of resolving textual ambiguities against the claim of constitutional right. It is far from clear what justifies such a presumption against claims of right. Nothing intrinsic in the nature of interpretation—if there is such a thing as the "nature" of interpretation—commands such a passive approach to ambiguity. This is a choice no less political than any other; it expresses antipathy to claims of the minority to rights against the majority. Those who would restrict claims of right to the values of 1789 specifically articulated in the Constitution turn a blind eye to social progress and eschew adaptation of overarching principles to changes of social circumstance.

Another, perhaps more sophisticated, response to the potential power of judicial interpretation stresses democratic theory: because ours is a government of the people's elected representatives, substantive value choices should by and large be left to them. This view emphasizes not the transcendent historical authority of the framers but the predominant contemporary authority of the elected branches of government. Yet it has similar consequences for the nature of proper judicial interpretation. Faith in the majoritarian process counsels restraint. Even under more expansive formulations of this approach, judicial review is appropriate only to the extent of ensuring that our democratic process functions smoothly. Thus, for example, we would protect freedom of speech merely to ensure that the people are heard by their representatives, rather than as a separate, substantive value. When, by contrast, society tosses up to the Supreme Court a dispute that would require invalidation of a legislature's substantive policy choice, the Court generally would stay its hand because the Constitution was meant as a plan of government and not as an embodiment of fundamental substantive values.

The view that all matters of substantive policy should be resolved through the majoritarian process has appeal under some circumstances, but I think it ultimately will not do. Unabashed enshrinement of majority would permit the imposition of a social caste system or wholesale confiscation of property so long as a majority of the authorized legislative body, fairly elected, approved. Our Constitution could not abide such a situation. It is the very purpose of a constitution—and particularly of the Bill of Rights—to declare certain values transcendent, beyond the reach of temporary political majorities. The majoritarian process cannot be expected to rectify claims of minority right that arise as a response to the outcomes of that very majoritarian process. As James Madison put it:

> The prescriptions in favor of liberty ought to be levelled against that quarter where the greatest danger lies, namely, that which possesses the highest prerogative of power. But this is not found in either the executive or legislative departments of Government, but in the body of the people, operating by the majority against the minority. (I Annals 437).

Faith in democracy is one thing, blind faith quite another. Those who drafted our Constitution understood the difference. One cannot read the text without admitting that it embodies substantive value choices; it places certain values beyond the power of any legislature. Obvious are the separation of powers; the privilege of the Writ of Habeas Corpus; prohibition of Bills of Attainder and ex post facto laws; prohibition of cruel and unusual punishments; the requirement of just compensation for official taking of property; the prohibition of laws tending to establish religion or enjoining the free exercise of religion; and, since the Civil War, the banishment of slavery and official race discrimination. With respect to at least such principles, we simply have not constituted ourselves as strict utilitarians. While the Constitution may be amended, such amendments require an immense effort by the people as a whole.

To remain faithful to the content of the Constitution, therefore, an approach to interpreting the text must account for the existence of these substantive value choices, and must accept the ambiguity inherent in the effort to apply them to modern circumstances. The Framers discerned fundamental principles through struggles against particular malefactions of the Crown; the struggle shapes the particular contours of the articulated principles. But our acceptance of the fundamental principles has not and should not bind us to those precise, at times anachronistic, contours. Successive generations of Americans have continued to respect these fundamental choices and adopt them as their own guide to evaluating quite different historical practices. Each generation has the choice to overrule or add to the fundamental principles enunciated by the Framers; the Constitution can be amended or it can be ignored. Yet with respect to its fundamental principles, the text has suffered neither fate. Thus, if I may borrow the words of an esteemed predecessor, Justice Robert Jackson, the burden of judicial interpretation is to translate "the majestic generalities of the Bill of Rights, conceived as part of the pattern of liberal government in the eighteenth century, into concrete restraints on officials dealing with the problems of the twentieth century." (Barnette, 319 U.S. at 639).

We current Justices read the Constitution in the only way that we can: as twentieth century Americans. We look to the history of the time of framing and to the intervening history of interpretation. But the ultimate question must be, what do the words of the text mean in our time. For the genius of the Constitution rests not in any static meaning it might have had in a world that is dead and gone, but in the adaptability of its great principles to cope with current problems and current needs. What the constitutional fundamentals meant to the wisdom of other times cannot be their measure to the vision of our time. Similarly, what those fundamentals mean for us, our descendants will learn, cannot be the measure to the vision of other time. This realization is not, I assure you, a novel one of my own creation. Permit me to quote from one of the opinions of our Court, *Weems v. United States*, 217 U.S. 349, written nearly a century ago:

> "Time works changes, brings into existence new conditions and purposes. Therefore, a principle, to be vital, must be capable of wider application than the mischief which gave it birth. This is peculiarly true of constitutions. They are not ephemeral enactments, designed to meet passing occasions. They are, to use the words of Chief Justice John Marshall, 'designed to approach immortality as nearly as human institutions can approach it.' The future is their care and provision for events of good and bad tendencies of which no prophecy can be made. In the application of a constitution, therefore, our contemplation cannot be only of what has been, but of what may be."

Interpretation must account for the transformative purpose of the text. Our Constitution was not intended to preserve a preexisting society but to make a new one, to put in place new principles that the prior political community had not sufficiently recognized. Thus, for example, when we interpret the Civil War Amendments to the charter—abolishing slavery, guaranteeing blacks equality under law, and guaranteeing blacks the right to vote—we must remember that those who put them in place had no desire to enshrine the status quo. Their goal was to make over their world, to eliminate all vestige of slave caste.

Having discussed at some length how I, as a Supreme Court Justice, interact with this text, I think it is time to turn to the fruits of this discourse. For the Constitution is a sublime oration on the dignity of man, a bold commitment by a people to the ideal of libertarian dignity protected through law. Some reflection is perhaps required before this can be seen.

The Constitution on its face is, in large measure, a structuring text, a blueprint for government. And when the text is not prescribing the form of government it is limiting the powers of that government. The original document, before addition of any of the amendments, does not speak primarily of the rights of man, but of the abilities and disabilities of government. When one reflects upon the text's preoccupation with the scope of government as well as its shape, however, one comes to understand that what this text is about is the relationship of the individual and the state. The text marks the metes and bounds of official authority and individual autonomy. When one studies the boundary that the text marks out, one gets a sense of the vision of the individual embodied in the Constitution.

As augmented by the Bill of Rights and the Civil War Amendments, this text is a sparkling vision of the supremacy of the human dignity of every individual. This vision is reflected in the very choice of democratic self-governance: the supreme value of a democracy is the presumed worth of each individual. And this vision manifests itself most dramatically in the specific prohibitions of the Bill of Rights, a term which I henceforth will apply to describe not only the original first eight amendments, but the Civil War amendments as well. It is a vision that has guided us as a people throughout our history, although the precise rules by which we have protected fundamental human dignity have been transformed over time in response to both transformations of social condition and evolution of our concepts of human dignity.

Until the end of the nineteenth century, freedom and dignity in our country found meaningful protection in the institution of real property. In a society still largely agricultural, a piece of land provided men not just with sustenance, but with the means of economic independence, a necessary precondition of political independence and expression. Not surprisingly, property relationships formed the heart of litigation and of legal practice, and lawyers and judges tended to think stable property relationships the highest aim of the law.

But the days when common law property relationships dominated litigation and legal practice are past. To a growing extent economic existence now depends on less certain relationships with government—licenses, employment, contracts, subsidies, unemployment benefits, tax exemptions, welfare and the like. Government participation in the economic existence of individuals is pervasive and deep. Administrative matters and other dealings with government are at the epicenter of the exploding law. We turn to government and to the law for controls which would never have been expected or tolerated before this century, when a man's answer to economic oppression or difficulty was to move two hundred miles west. Now hundreds of thousands of Americans live entire lives without any real prospect of the dignity and autonomy that ownership of real property could confer. Protection of the human dignity of such citizens requires a much modified view of the proper relationship of individual and state.

In general, problems of the relationship of the citizen with government have multiplied and thus have engendered some of the most important constitutional issues of the day. As government acts ever more deeply upon those areas of our lives once marked "private," there is an even greater need to see that individual rights are not curtailed or cheapened in the interest of what may temporarily appear to be the "public good." And as government continues in its role of provider for so many of our disadvantaged citizens, there is an even greater need to ensure that government act with integrity and consistency in its dealings with these citizens. To put this another way, the possibilities for collision between government activity and individual rights will increase as the power and authority of government itself expands, and this growth, in turn, heightens the need for constant vigilance at the collision points. If our free society is to endure, those who govern must recognize human dignity and accept the enforcement of constitutional limitations on their power conceived by the Framers to be necessary to preserve that dignity and the air of freedom which is our proudest heritage. Such recognition will not come from a technical understanding of the organs of government, or the new forms of wealth they administer. It requires something different, something deeper—a personal confrontation with the well-springs of our society. Solutions of constitutional questions from that perspective have become the great challenge of the modern era. All the talk in the last half-decade about shrinking the government does not alter this reality or the challenge it imposes. The modern activist state is a concomitant of the complexity of modern society; it is inevitably with us. We must meet the challenge rather than wish it were not before us.

The challenge is essentially, of course, one to the capacity of our constitutional structure to foster and protect the freedom, the dignity, and the rights of all persons within our borders, which it is the great design of the Constitution to secure. During the time of my public service this challenge has largely taken shape within the confines of the interpretive question whether the specific guarantees of the Bill of Rights operate as restraints on the power of state government. We recognize the Bill of Rights as the primary source of express information as to what is meant by constitutional liberty. The safeguards enshrined in it are deeply etched in the foundation of America's freedoms. Each is a protection with centuries of history behind it, often dearly bought with the blood and lives of people determined to prevent oppression by their rulers. The first eight Amendments, however, were added to the Constitution to operate solely against federal power. It was not until the Thirteenth and Fourteenth Amendments were added, in 1865 and 1868, in response to a demand for national protection against abuses of state power, that the Constitution could be interpreted to require application of the first eight Amendments to the states.

It was in particular that Fourteenth Amendment's guarantee that no person be deprived of life, liberty or property without process of law that led us to apply many of the specific guarantees of the Bill of Rights to the states. In my judgment, Justice Cardozo best captured the reasoning that brought us to such decisions when he described what the Court has done as a process by which the guarantees "have been taken over from the earlier articles of the federal bill of rights and brought within the Fourteenth Amendment by a process of absorption . . . [that] has had its source in the belief that neither liberty nor justice would exist if [those guarantees] . . . were sacrificed." (Palko, 302 U.S., at 326). But this process of absorption was neither swift nor steady. As late as 1922, only the Fifth Amendment guarantee of just compensation for official taking of property had been given force against the states. Between then and 1956, only the First Amendment guarantees of speech and conscience and the Fourth Amendment ban of unreasonable searches and seizures had been incorporated—the latter, however, without the exclusionary rule to give it force. As late as 1961, I could stand before a distinguished assemblage of the bar at New York University's James Madison Lecture and list the following guarantees that had not been thought to be sufficiently fundamental to the protection of human dignity so as to be enforced against the states: the prohibition of cruel and unusual punishments, the right against self-incrimination, the right to assistance to counsel in a criminal trial, the right to confront witnesses, the right to compulsory process, the right not to be placed in jeopardy of life or limb more than once upon accusation of a crime, the right not to have illegally obtained evidence introduced at a criminal trial, and the right to a jury of one's peers.

The history of the quarter century following that Madison Lecture need not be told in great detail. Suffice it to say that each of the guarantees listed above has been recognized as a fundamental aspect of ordered liberty. Of course, the above catalogue encompasses only the rights of the criminally accused, those caught, rightly or wrongly, in the maw of the criminal justice system. But it has been well said that there is no better test of a society than how it treats those accused of transgressing against it. Indeed, it is because we recognize that incarceration strips a man of his dignity that we demand strict adherence to fair procedure and proof of guilt beyond a reasonable doubt before taking such a drastic step. These requirements are, as Justice Harlan once said, "bottomed on a fundamental value determination of our society that it is far worse to convict an innocent man than to let a guilty man go free." (Winship, 397 U.S., at 372). There is no worse injustice than wrongly to strip a man of his dignity. And our adherence to the constitutional vision of human dignity is so strict that even after convicting a person according to these stringent standards, we demand that his dignity be infringed only to the extent appropriate to the crime and never by means of wanton infliction of pain or deprivation. I interpret the Constitution plainly to embody these fundamental values.

Of course the constitutional vision of human dignity has, in this past quarter century, infused more than our decisions about the criminal process. Recognition of the principle of "one person, one vote" as a constitutional one redeems the promise of self-governance by affirming the essential dignity of every citizen in the right to equal participation in the democratic process. Recognition of so-called "new property" rights in those receiving government entitlements affirms the essential dignity of the least fortunate among us by demanding that government treat with decency, integrity and consistency those dependent on its benefits for their very survival. After all, a legislative majority initially decides to create governmental entitlements; the Constitution's Due Process Clause merely provides protection for entitlements thought necessary by society as a whole. Such due process rights prohibit government from imposing the devil's bargain of bartering away human dignity in exchange for human sustenance. Likewise, recognition of full equality for women—equal protection of laws—ensures that gender has no bearing on claims of human dignity.

Recognition of broad and deep rights of expression and of conscience reaffirm the vision of human dignity in many ways. They too redeem the promise of self-governance by facilitating—indeed demanding—robust, uninhibited and wide-open debate on issues of public importance. Such public debate is, of course, vital to the development and dissemination of political ideas. As importantly, robust public discussion is the crucible in which personal political convictions are forged. In our democracy, such discussion is a political duty; it is the essence of self government. The constitutional vision of human dignity rejects the possibility of political orthodoxy imposed from above; it respects the right of each individual to form and to express political judgments, however far they may deviate from the mainstream, and however unsettling they might be to the powerful or the elite. Recognition of these rights of expression and conscience also frees up the private space for both intellectual and spiritual development free of government dominance, either blatant or subtle. Justice Brandeis put it so well sixty years ago when he wrote: "Those who won our independence believed that the final end of the State was to make men free to develop their faculties; and that in its government the deliberative forces should prevail over the arbitrary. They valued liberty both as an end and as a means." (Whitney, 274 U.S., at 375).

I do not mean to suggest that we have in the last quarter century achieved a comprehensive definition of the constitutional ideal of human dignity. We are still striving toward that goal, and doubtless it will be an eternal quest. For if the interaction of this Justice and the constitutional text over the years confirms any single proposition, it is that the demands of human dignity will never cease to evolve.

Indeed, I cannot in good conscience refrain from mention of one grave and crucial respect in which we continue, in my judgment, to fall short of the constitutional vision of human dignity. It is in our continued tolerance of State-administered execution as a form of punishment. I make it a practice not to comment on the constitutional issues that come before the Court, but my position on this issue, of course, has been for some time fixed and immutable. I think I can venture some thoughts on this particular subject without transgressing my usual guideline too severely.

As I interpret the Constitution, capital punishment is under all circumstances cruel and unusual punishment prohibited by the

Eighth and Fourteenth Amendments. This is a position of which I imagine you are not unaware. Much discussion of the merits of capital punishment has in recent years focused on the potential arbitrariness that attends its administration, and I have no doubt that such arbitrariness is a grave wrong. But for me, the wrong of capital punishment transcends such procedural issues. As I have said in my opinions, I view the Eighth Amendment's prohibition of cruel and unusual punishments as embodying to a unique degree moral principles that substantively restrain the punishments our civilized society may impose on those persons who transgress its laws. Foremost among the moral principles recognized in our cases and inherent in the prohibition is the primary principle that the State, even as it punishes, must treat its citizens in a manner consistent with their intrinsic worth as human beings. A punishment must not be so severe as to be utterly and irreversibly degrading to the very essence of human dignity. Death for whatever crime and under all circumstances is a truly awesome punishment. The calculated killing of a human being by the State involves, by its very nature, an absolute denial of the executed person's humanity. The most vile murder does not, in my view, release the State from constitutional restraints on the destruction of human dignity. Yet an executed person has lost the very right to have rights, now or ever. For me, then, the fatal constitutional infirmity of capital punishment is that it treats members of the human race as nonhumans, as objects to be toyed with and discarded. It is, indeed, "cruel and unusual." It is thus inconsistent with the fundamental premise of the Clause that even the most base criminal remains a human being possessed of some potential, at least, for common human dignity.

This is an interpretation to which a majority of my fellow Justices—not to mention, it would seem, a majority of my fellow countrymen—does not subscribe. Perhaps you find my adherence to it, and my recurrent publication of it, simply contrary, tiresome, or quixotic. Or perhaps you see in it a refusal to abide by the judicial principle of *stare decisis:* obedience to precedent. In my judgment, however, the unique interpretive role of the Supreme Court with respect to the Constitution demands some flexibility with respect to the call of *stare decisis*. Because we are the last word on the meaning of the Constitution, our views must be subject to revision over time, or the Constitution falls captive, again, to the anachronistic views of long-gone generations. I mentioned earlier the judge's role in seeking out the community's interpretation of the Constitutional text. Yet, again in my judgment, when a Justice perceives an interpretation of the text to have departed so far from its essential meaning, that

Justice is bound, by a larger constitutional duty to the community, to expose the departure and point toward a different path. On this issue, the death penalty, I hope to embody a community striving for human dignity for all, although perhaps not yet arrived.

You have doubtless observed that this description of my personal encounter with the constitutional text has in large portion been a discussion of public developments in constitutional doctrine over the last quarter century. That, as I suggested at the outset, is inevitable because my interpretive career has demanded a public reading of the text. This public encounter with the text, however, has been a profound source of personal inspiration. The vision of human dignity embodied there is deeply moving. It is timeless. It has inspired Americans for two centuries, and it will continue to inspire as it continues to evolve. That evolutionary process is inevitable and, indeed, it is the true interpretive genius of the text.

If we are to be as a shining city upon a hill, it will be because of our ceaseless pursuit of the constitutional ideal of human dignity. For the political and legal ideals that form the foundation of much that is best in American institutions—ideals jealously preserved and guarded throughout our history—still form the vital force in creative political thought and activity within the nation today. As we adapt our institutions to the ever-changing conditions of national and international life, those ideals of human dignity—liberty and justice for all individuals—will continue to inspire and guide us because they are entrenched in our Constitution. The Constitution with its Bill of Rights thus has a bright future, as well as a glorious past, for its spirit is inherent in the aspirations of our people.